MW00438221

Quiet Moments
with Bill Bright

Quiet Moments
with Bill Bright

Compiled by the editors of
NewLife Publications, a ministry of
Campus Crusade for Christ International

SERVANT PUBLICATIONS
ANN ARBOR, MICHIGAN

Vine Books is an imprint of Servant Publications especially designed to serve
evangelical Christians.

Published by Servant Publications
P.O. Box 8617
Ann Arbor, Michigan 48107

Cover design: Left Coast Design, Portland, Oregon
Photographs on the dust jacket, and pages 15, 26, and 47 are used by permission of
New Life Publications, a Ministry of Campus Crusade for Christ. The publisher has
been unsuccessful in efforts to locate the copyright holders of the photographs on
pages 67, 80, 99, and 131 and will gladly give credit in future editions to photogra-
phers who notify the publisher.

99 00 01 02 10 9 8 7 6 5 4 3 2 1

Printed in the United States of America
ISBN 1-56955-167-7

LIBRARY OF CONGRESS CATALOGING-IN-PUBLICATION DATA

Bright, Bill.
    Quiet moments with Bill Bright.
       p.   cm.
    ISBN 1-56955-167-7 (alk. paper)
    1. Meditations.   I. Title.
BV4832.2.B726   1999
242—dc21

                                                99-32268
                                                CIP

1 – The Secrets of His Promises

What a wonderful way to start a new day—reaffirming our friendship with God and the fact that His promises are sure (see Ps 25:14). He is the Friend who desires an intimate relationship with His children. Think of that! A friendship with our wonderful Creator who spoke and a hundred billion galaxies were flung into space. The One who designed creation so intricately that every microscopic molecule has its place and purpose.

Reflect for a moment on His majestic power, His total sovereignty, and His limitless knowledge. The fact that Almighty God lives within us overwhelms me. What a privilege to spend time with Him each day!

One of the delights of my life is to walk with God moment by moment and know that He is closer to me than the air that I breathe. During quiet times of worship, He discloses profound insights in His Word, which He does for all who reverence Him.

Each of us can experience an adventure of discovering God's promises. They help us depend more upon God and experience the supernatural life that only He can give.

Take a few quiet moments in the morning or during a break in your day to meditate on a Bible passage and prayerfully apply what you read. I am sure that you will find that a deeper friendship with God which will enrich your life and help you live above the daily grind.

2 – The Bible's No. 1 Promise

On Easter Sunday 1990, I stood in the Palace of Congress inside the Kremlin walls and presented the message of God's love and forgiveness to 6,000 Russian people. An estimated 250 million people watched by television and 100 million listened by radio.

What a privilege! I spoke to millions of Russians who had been denied the gospel for seventy-three years. I shared with them the most glorious message ever given: John 3:16:

God: He is the all-powerful, loving, sovereign, holy, wise, compassionate God.

So loved: His love is unconditional and inexhaustible.

The world: This includes every person who inhabits earth.

He gave His one and only Son: God freely gave us His more priceless gift, Jesus.

That whoever: That means you and me.

Believes in Him: To believe means accepting by faith that Jesus is the Son of God and Savior of the world.

Shall not perish: When we receive Jesus as Savior, we cannot be separated from God.

But have eternal life: This not only includes our heavenly life but also our earthly life, where we experience the everlasting life of the risen Savior.

3 – The Fullness of the Spirit

An enthusiastic couple traveled from Chicago to Arrowhead Springs, California, to share their experience with me. "Our lives were dramatically changed after watching one of your filmed lectures on 'How to Be Filled with the Holy Spirit.' He has helped us overcome great difficulties in our lives and given us more joy than we ever imagined."

I have seen many believers discover the same dramatic results experienced by this remarkable couple. No one can live the Christian life without the power of the Holy Spirit. The disciples were with Jesus for more than three years. They witnessed the most godly life ever lived. Yet when Jesus needed them during His crucifixion, Peter denied Him, and the others deserted Him.

Jesus knew His disciples were fruitless, quarreling, self-centered men. That is why He promised to send the Holy Spirit to guide them. When the Holy Spirit came, the disciples were filled with power and became courageous and bold and served the Lord with all their hearts.

"Be filled" in Ephesians 5:18 means to be constantly and continually filled, controlled, and empowered with the Holy Spirit every moment of every day. Just as we received Christ by faith, so we are filled with the Holy Spirit by faith. Ask God to fill you with His Holy Spirit.

When we choose, as an act of our will, to yield our lives to God, the Holy Spirit gives us power to live victoriously and supernaturally.

4 – Love Without Limit

One day I opened my Bible to the prayer of Jesus found in John 17:22,23. In this passage, He is talking to God His Father. As I was reading, I leaped from my chair in amazement. I realized that God loves us as much as He loves His one and only Son! What is more, He loves us unconditionally. He loves us simply because He is a God of love, not because we are good or worthy.

Jesus' death on the cross for our sins is the ultimate expression of God's limitless love. This love stems from the character of the person loving, not the worthiness of the object of that love. God's love is pictured in 1 Corinthians 13. This chapter describes the kind of love that Jesus demonstrated when He lived on earth as a man.

Jesus' example is a guideline for us to love as God loves. When Jesus comes to live His life through us, God's love flows through us, enabling us to love others supernaturally. Read the Gospels with this in mind. Note the times Jesus helped people when He was tired or when it was inconvenient. See how He reacted when people treated Him unfairly. Think about how He sacrificed His rights as you read the story of His crucifixion. Then thank God often for His great love.

5 – Abundant Life

What were you like before you were introduced to Jesus Christ? Before I received Him as my Savior, I was a happy pagan, committed to the "good life" of materialism. I owned my own business and worked long hours to enjoy success. My first priority was to make a lot of money, live in an expensive home, and travel the world. But as I came to know the God of Scripture, I surrendered myself completely to His authority.

Did I lose anything? Absolutely not. The Lord has given me far more than I could have ever accomplished for myself. I have incredible peace, riches awaiting me in heaven, and God's supernatural joy. I have a loving wife, wonderful children and grandchildren, and a ministry which keeps surprising and challenging me every day.

Jesus gives abundant life to those who walk in faith and obedience to God (see Jn 10:10). If you are not experiencing such a life, you can have it today, tomorrow, and the rest of your days—no matter what your circumstances. You start by getting to know God—who He is, what He is like, and the benefits we enjoy when we belong to His family.

Would I trade my old life as an unbeliever for what I have now? Never! And I am sure you will not either once you experience the abundant life Jesus gives as you live in faith and obedience.

6 – The Power of Prayer

Years ago when Campus Crusade for Christ's headquarters was located at beautiful Arrowhead Springs, California, a wildfire swept through the area. Many buildings, including the bungalow where my wife, Vonette, and I lived, came perilously close to being engulfed in flames. Vonette and I were in San Diego when word came at noon that our headquarters staff had been evacuated. About 2:30, urgent word came that the flames had engulfed the campus. Claiming John 14:14, we got on our knees and prayed that God would turn the winds.

At the same time, headquarters staff began praying that God would turn the ninety-mile-per-hour winds away from the buildings. Around 2:30, they looked out the window at the flag snapping in the wind. Suddenly, it began to pivot and made a 180-degree turn. They were awestruck at what God had done before their very eyes!

Vonette and I heard that several buildings had burned. Since our home stood on the edge of the campus, it was more vulnerable than other buildings. On our arrival, we learned that God had miraculously answered our prayers and preserved our home.

We can believe God for great and mighty things. Although sometimes He says no or wait, He gives us sufficient strength to face our trials. When He says yes, He gives us more than we could ever think to ask.

7 – Keeping Sin-Accounts Short

Before I became a Christian, the subject of the blood of Jesus offended me. Then one day as I studied Hebrews 10, I found myself on my knees, overwhelmed with a deep sense of gratitude. Because of Christ's blood, my sins are forgiven forever. Nothing I can do will ever take away that forgiveness. I can lose fellowship with God, but I will never lose my relationship with Him.

If Christ has sacrificed so much for me, what can I do in return? Cooperate with Him in His process of making me holy. This process is accelerated through keeping my sin-accounts short.

I call the practice of keeping short accounts with God "Spiritual Breathing"—exhaling through confessing sin and inhaling by appropriating the fullness of God's Holy Spirit by faith. Because of our sin nature, each of us has the desire to run our own life. If you retake control of your life through sin, breathe spiritually. First, exhale by confession. First John 1:9 says, "If we confess our sins, he is faithful and just and will forgive us our sins and purify us from all unrighteousness" (NIV). Next, inhale by appropriating the fullness of God's Spirit by faith. Ask Him to empower you according to His command to "be filled with the Spirit" (Eph 5:18).

Today when I partake of communion, I find myself again in tears of gratitude as I remember what Christ has done for me.

8 – The Importance of Humility

Do you have a favorite verse that God has brought to your mind many times? For years, I have claimed 2 Chronicles 7:14. My focus has been on our need to humble ourselves before God and turn from sin.

This is why in the summer of 1994, I began a forty-day spiritual fast. I felt called to seek God's face for myself. In addition, the spiritual condition of our country lay heavily on my heart. I also wanted the Lord to refresh me and the Campus Crusade for Christ staff in His Spirit and to rekindle our first love for Him (see Rv 2:1-7). I prayed that the Holy Spirit would spur us on in our mission to help introduce a billion people to Christ.

During my fast, I enjoyed the Lord's presence in a wonderful, special way. I discerned for the first time that the only Christian discipline which meets all the conditions of 2 Chronicles 7:14 is sincere fasting with prayer.

What is your greatest need? Do you have a sin that constantly tempts you? Do you have a deep concern for our country? I encourage you to seek God today. King David declared that he humbled himself through fasting. Perhaps you, too, would like to begin fasting and praying. I assure you that God will honor your humility by renewing your life and vision.

9 – Foundation for Holy Living

I enjoy Martin Luther's explanation of how to study the Bible:

> Search the Bible as a whole, shaking the whole tree. Read it rapidly, as you would any other book. Then shake every limb—study book after book.
>
> Then shake every branch, giving attention to the chapters when they do not break the sense. Then shake each twig, by a careful study of the paragraphs and sentences. And you will be rewarded if you will look under each leaf, by searching the meaning of the words.

Every time we read God's Word carefully, we build up our storehouse of faith. When we memorize the Bible, we make God's words available at a moment's notice. As we study or teach a Sunday school lesson or hear a sermon on the Word, we grow spiritually.

How many limbs have you shaken this month? How many leaves have you looked under?

I encourage you to make God's Word the foundation of your life. Apply its principles to your marriage and your family (see Eph 5:21–6:4). Apply its instructions in your business (see Prv 10:4-6; 11:1; Lk 12:15-21; Rom 12:17,18). Use its wisdom to plan your finances (see Lk 6:38; 1 Cor 16:2; Rom 13:8).

Use a Bible tool such as a topical index to receive more help in the problems or decisions you face. Rely on God's wisdom to enable you to do what is right.

10 – Joy in Sowing Tears

Fifty years ago, I heard Dr. Oswald Smith, well-known Christian pastor and missionary statesman, challenge about a thousand singles to commit their lives to helping introduce others to Christ. He asked each of us to place our names on a country and claim it for the Lord as God would lead. I put my name on the Soviet Union and began praying for its people. After I married Vonette, she joined me in prayer. Over the years, God gave us a special love and burden for the Soviet people.

Today, a tremendous spiritual harvest is taking place in what was once known as the "Evil Empire." I have had the privilege of helping present the gospel to tens of millions of Russians via television and radio and in person. In cooperation with other Christian ministries, Campus Crusade has helped to train thousands of teachers to present the gospel to school children all over Russia and Eastern Europe.

Where does the compassion for souls originate? In the heart of God. It comes as we are controlled and empowered by the Holy Spirit.

How long has it been since you shed tears over those who do not know our Savior? Are you allowing God to use you to introduce others to Christ? In Psalm 126:5,6, God promises that when we sow the precious seed of His Word in tears, we will reap a spiritual harvest.

UCLA Ministry, 1951-52

11 – Spiritual Riches

Consider the contrast between these two people. A wealthy Christian woman panicked when the stock market dropped and she lost almost a million dollars. Although she had tens of millions in reserve, she was terrified that she would die a pauper. She had never discovered the freedom of "giving and receiving" in a trust relationship with God.

A short time later, a businessman called me long distance to tell me how excited he was about the way God was blessing his new business venture. He had decided to give all the profits—potentially millions—toward helping reach the world for Christ.

God has a different method from that of the world for gaining riches. Jesus promises: "If you give you will get! Your gift will return to you in full and overflowing measure, pressed down, shaken together to make room for more, and running over. Whatever measure you uses to give—large or small—will be used to measure what is given back to you" (Lk 6:38, TLB). The greatest way we can give is by using our finances to help introduce others to Jesus.

Whether you have one hundred dollars or one million dollars, ask God to show you how you can help reach the world for Christ. Look for a worthy project to support regularly along with your commitment to your church. Give more than you are capable of fulfilling with your present income. Then observe how God blesses you.

12 – Children of God

My wife, Vonette, had been active in the church since she was a little girl. When I began dating her, I assumed that she was a Christian. But during our engagement, I realized she had never received Christ as Savior, though she was a very moral, religious person.

Because of our emotional involvement, I hesitated to press her to receive Christ. I was afraid she would go through the motions just to please me. That certainly would not make her a child of God. So I asked the Lord to send someone who could introduce Vonette to Christ. He clearly led me to call upon a good friend, the late Dr. Henrietta Mears, who had played such a vital role in my own spiritual growth.

One day at Forest Home, a Christian conference center in California, Dr. Mears talked with Vonette. "Receiving Christ," she explained, "is simply a matter of turning your life—your will, emotion, and intellect—completely over to Him."

Hearing this, Vonette asked Jesus to forgive her sins and come into her life as Savior and Lord. At that moment, she became a child of God.

In John 1:12, God promises that we have the right to become part of His family when we trust in Jesus. I encourage you to search God's Word for other benefits which He gives His sons and daughters. And enjoy your intimate relationship with your loving, heavenly Father!

13 – Sound Mind Principle

God has promised that we can find His will for our lives. A helpful approach to knowing God's will is what I call the "sound mind principle" of Scripture. Second Timothy 1:7 records: "God has not given us a spirit of fear, but of power and of love and of a sound mind" (NKJV). This verse promises us a well-balanced mind—one that is under control of the Holy Spirit. Although God often leads us through impressions, He generally expects us to use our "sound minds." Instead of relying only on emotional impressions, the Spirit-filled Christian determines God's wisdom and direction through prayer and the study of God's Word.

For example, when you have an important decision to make:

1. Ask the Lord to cleanse you of your sin and to fill you with His Spirit.
2. Take a sheet of paper and list all the positive and negative factors in your situation.
3. Search God's Word to see what it says about the matter—directly and indirectly.
4. Seek the counsel of godly, knowledgeable people.
5. Make your decision on the basis of what seems obvious, unless God specifically leads you to the contrary.

Then rest on His promise to make His perfect will known to you.

14 – Exalting a Nation

Daniel Webster wrote of the importance of national godliness:

The moral principles and precepts contained in the Scriptures ought to form the basis of all our civil constitutions and laws. All the miseries and evils which men suffer from—vice, crime, ambition, injustice, oppression, slavery, and war—proceed from their despising or neglecting the precepts contained in the Bible.

Proverbs 14:34 (TLB) says, "Godliness exalts a nation, but sin is a reproach to any people." Our nation became great because it was founded on biblical principles. But today we are violating God's laws and reeling from the effects of violent crime, rampant divorce, sexual promiscuity, and other sins. We clearly see the consequences of ignoring God's laws.

What can we do to turn the tide of this evil? You can exalt America through your godly life. First Timothy 2:1, 2 reminds us to pray for our leaders so we can live in peace and quietness. That includes all those in authority, from our local precinct to the White House. We can also write letters and make personal appointments to communicate God's love to these officials.

It is vital for every Christian to live a life of godliness and to pray for our elected officials. If we do our part, we will see America return to its biblical foundation and experience God's blessing.

15 – Surprised by Mongolia

Recently, someone asked me, "In the past few years, which country surprised you most when it opened its doors to the gospel?" My answer, "Mongolia."

What a miracle that the secular government of that country requested our staff to show the *JESUS* film to their leadership. At the time of the premiere showing, we knew of only twelve believers in the entire nation. Since then, the film has been featured in all the theaters and in many schools. Tens of thousands of Mongolians have indicated decisions to receive Christ as Savior. The leaders, right up to the prime minister and president, are experiencing a dramatic shift in the way they view the world.

Similar changes are happening all over the world. Throughout Eastern Europe, Africa, and Latin America, millions are turning to Christ. The largest evangelical church in the world is in Asia.

Matthew 24:14 (TLB) records, "The Good News about the Kingdom will be preached throughout the whole world, so that all nations will hear it, and then ... finally, the end will come." I applaud every effort to warn Christians and nonbelievers to be ready for our Lord's return. Jesus will come again and has delayed His return so that more people might have a chance to hear the gospel. What a day of ecstasy, excitement, and awe that day will be!

16 – Spiritual Multiplication

One day, a Campus Crusade staff member handed me a copy of *Sports Illustrated* that had a cover picture of the Heisman Trophy winner. He said proudly, "I'd like to introduce you to your great-grandson."

Mystified, I asked, "What do you mean?"

"You led Jim to Christ; Jim led me to Christ; and I led Steve [the Heisman Trophy winner] to Christ."

What a joy to see God's wonder-working power in this chain reaction in what I call "spiritual multiplication."

The most important commands our Lord has given to us are: "Follow Me, and I will make you fishers of men" (Mt 4:19, NASB); and "Go therefore and make disciples of all the nations" (Mt 28:19, NASB). In other words, Jesus commands us to teach others the things He taught us. These commands are the basis of spiritual multiplication.

When we obey God by multiplying spiritually, we often experience more fulfillment than we get from our own ministry of introducing others to Christ. For example, whenever my sons, Zac and Brad, or others whom I have discipled through the years get excited about someone they led to Christ, I receive much more pleasure and delight than if I had introduced the person to Christ myself.

By investing your life in helping others receive Christ and train them to lead their friends to Christ, you will help people you have never met experience the abundant life which Jesus gives.

17 – Maturity—in His Timing

Unfortunately, and tragically, many Christians never pass the baby or childhood stages. Think of the heartache and sorrow God experiences when He looks upon those of His children who have never matured though they have been Christians for many years.

Martha, a new Christian, approached me with this question, "With all my heart I want to be a woman of God, but I do not experience the consistency of Galatians 5:22, 23 in my life. What is wrong?"

Maybe you are asking the same question. If so, it will be helpful for you to understand that the Christian life is a life of growth. Just as in our physical lives we begin as babies and progress through childhood into adolescence, young adulthood, and mature adulthood, so it is in out spiritual lives.

The Holy Spirit takes up residence within every believer at the moment of new birth. The growth process is greatly accelerated when a believer consciously yields himself to the lordship of Christ and the filling of the Holy Spirit. A believer who is empowered by the Holy Spirit, who is a faithful student of God's Word, and who has learned to trust and obey God, can pass through the various stages of spiritual growth and become a mature Christian within a brief period of time. Some Spirit-led Christians demonstrate more of the fruit of the Spirit within one year than others who have been untaught, uncommitted believers for fifty years.

18 – Sunrise!

As a senior citizen, I know what it means to have aches and pains. Each of them is a reminder that I am closer to my heavenly home. In fact, I am eagerly waiting for the day when Jesus changes my address—to heaven. John 14:1-6 describes this moment.

I am deeply moved by the dying experience of D.L. Moody. A few hours before leaving this earth for his heavenly mansion, he caught a glimpse of the glory in store for him. Awakening from a sleep, he said, "Earth recedes, heaven opens before me. If this is death, it is sweet. There is no valley here. God is calling here. God is calling me, and I must go."

His son stood by his bedside. "No, no, father, you are dreaming."

"No," Moody said, "I am not dreaming. I have been within the gates."

A short time passed, then he seemed to be in a final struggle with death. But he managed to say, "This is my triumph. This is my coronation day. It is glorious!"

Are you eagerly anticipating the day when Jesus fulfills His promise and takes you to your heavenly home? Are you excited about receiving a new body that will never decay? That moment will be truly a sunrise—the beginning of your eternal life in the presence of our Lord.

19 – God's Perfect Words

A story is told of a young woman who started reading a famous novel because her friends highly recommended it. As she read the first few pages, she found the story dry and uninteresting. After a few chapters, she put it down to read something else. When her friends encouraged her to keep trying, she came back to read it again. But the book just did not interest her.

Then one day she met the author of the novel. They began dating, and she fell in love with him. Now she could hardly wait to read the novel. It became the most exciting book she had ever read, because she had discovered the wonderful person who wrote the book.

Many years ago, I had a similar experience. During my years of skepticism and agnosticism, I found the Bible dry and difficult to read. I believed it was filled with errors and inconsistencies. After I received Jesus Christ as my Savior, I began to read the Bible again. Now it was a completely different book—filled with exciting, life-changing truths! All the errors and contradictions had disappeared.

Why the difference? Because I had fallen in love with the Author, our Lord Jesus Christ. Now His words were beautiful to me. I enjoyed reading them everyday. First Peter 1:23 describes the Word of God as living and enduring. As you too get to know the Author, you will have a deeper love for God's perfect words.

20 – Great Boasting

The other day, Vonette and I were enjoying the rides at an amusement park with our grandson. He and Vonette decided to ride the train while I sat on a bench watching them. All kinds of people stood in line around me, waiting for their turn.

I leaned back and closed my eyes, meditating on the wonderful attributes of God: His sovereignty and power, His love and faithfulness. Suddenly, I was overcome with the joy of the Lord and dissolved into tears of praise and thanksgiving to this great God who made Himself so real to me. The parents around me were so involved with their children that they did not pay any attention to me. So the Lord and I had a wonderful time together.

I thought about how the Lord delights in doing good and about His holiness. He also promises to delight in us when we boast about Him to others. So how do we boast in the Lord? When we give Him credit for the good things in our lives, we exalt Him. When we praise Him aloud, we glorify Him (see Jer 9:24).

We can also boast in the Lord through our lifestyle. In the books we read. The music we play. The television programs we watch. Whatever we do that brings glory to God boasts of our love for Him. And He delights in that, too.

Bill Bright with Rafer Johnson, 1960.

21 – Place of Privilege

When former President Reagan was in office, Vonette and I were invited to the White House for a state dinner. At first, we did not realize what a unique opportunity this was. We assumed that all congressmen and cabinet members regularly attend these events. But we soon found out that these invitations are rare and few people ever receive more than one.

What a privilege! Vonette and I were meeting with President Reagan and his wife, Nancy, and the head of state from a foreign country. The Marine band and color guard performed magnificently. We were able to talk with other guests as well.

Although I deeply admire President Reagan and other presidents whom I have met, knowing them cannot compare with having a relationship with Jesus Christ, the King of Kings, and Lord of Lords. I do not need an appointment to talk to the Creator of the universe. I can come into His presence any hour of the day or night.

How did we receive this honor? According to Romans 5:2, our faith brought us to this place of highest privilege. What are some of the benefits that come with this unfathomable blessing?

First, we are justified—considered righteous in God's sight. Second, we live in His favor. Third, we have the prospect of even higher and richer blessings when we get to heaven. Let us humbly thank God for giving us such favor.

22 – In His Thoughts

Are you experiencing an intimate relationship with God? You can. Psalm 139:17,18 says that God is always thinking about us.

My sons, Zac and Brad, have helped me understand in some small measure the truth of this promise. They are never far from my thoughts. During a single day, I will lift them up in prayer many times. Now that they are married, I also remember to pray for my daughters-in-law and my grandchildren. When I remember how much God thinks about me, I want to do the same for them.

My love for my sons is limited, but God's love is limitless. He always wants what is best for me.

What an encouraging thought. God, who possesses all power, loves me enough to constantly think about me. When I wake up in the morning, His thoughts are on me. If I have an important meeting to attend, He sees me through it. If I am flying in an airplane, He is there. When I am asleep, He watches over me. No matter where I am or what I do, God is always present in my life.

When I allow Him to do so, He talks to me. He expresses His love, wisdom, and grace through His Word, through divine impressions, and the counsel of godly friends. His eyes search throughout the whole earth so that He can use His strength on my behalf (see 2 Chr 16:9).

23 – A Holy Life

Did you know that you can live a holy life? We can if we follow God's Word. That is the clear message of Psalm 119:9. And if that is true—and I have no doubt about it—then how can I be sure to follow God's Word?

I have found three simple steps that help me become so immersed in God's Word that I can recognize and battle temptation in my life.

First, I begin each day determining to know and obey God's Word. I remind myself that I cannot obey His Word if I am not familiar with it. But when I know God's Word, I can combat Satan and his influences.

Second, I make time daily for reading and studying the Bible. In a day when immorality is rampant, we need guidelines on how to keep our life pure. There is no better way to accomplish this than by dedicating time out each day to read and study the Bible.

Third, I memorize God's Word. Psalm 119:11 say that God's words will hold us back from our sin. When we memorize the Word, we can use it in times of need and to help us avoid temptation.

I encourage you to begin by reading, studying, and memorizing portions of Psalm 119. Master other portions of Scripture that also mean a lot to you. Then, whenever you encounter a temptation, use what you have learned from God's Word to resist doing evil.

24 – Renewed Strength

To keep in touch with Campus Crusade for Christ leaders on every continent, I have traveled millions of miles over the years. One three-month schedule took me on hops between twenty cities in seven different countries, including speaking at four Christmas conferences within a couple of days. This did not count numerous side trips. I could not do half of what I do if God did not give me His supernatural strength through the Holy Spirit. Only He has enabled me to keep up this pace for more than forty years.

An anonymous observer once said, "An hour in prayer can give the believer enough power to overcome the second most powerful force in the universe—whatever that is."

God's Word gives us many precious promises that confirm the truth of this wise observation. For example, Isaiah 40:31, (TLB) says, "They that wait upon the Lord shall renew their strength." Whenever it seems like my day is too full or whenever I do not have enough energy to accomplish a huge task, I claim this promise.

Renewed strength—spiritual strength, God's strength—is all we need to face each problem, difficulty, testing, or trial that confronts us. I encourage you to let God take over whatever you face and let His mighty strength carry you through the challenge of each day.

25 – A Hundred Times Over

God will return to you and me a hundred times over what we invest for Him and His kingdom (see Mk 10:29,30). I have found this to be absolutely true.

In 1951, Vonette and I surrendered our lives totally and completely to the Lord Jesus. I was beginning to see great material success through my business. But because we loved the Lord and felt Him leading us into full-time ministry, we gave up the opportunity to make and accumulate material wealth.

As I look back, we have received one hundred times more than we sacrificed that Sunday afternoon. It is conceivable that I might have made enough so that I could give millions of dollars to the cause of Christ in my lifetime. With hard work and faithfulness, I might have introduced many thousands to Christ.

Today, however, when I think of the annual budget of Campus Crusade and the tens of millions of people who have come into God's kingdom because of our organization, I get so excited over what God has done and is still doing in my life.

Of course, the greatest benefit has been the wonderful adventure of walking with God all these years. And on top of this, I receive eternal life! Put your trust in God's promise to reward your sacrifice for Him and experience His bountiful blessings.

26 – Unshaken in Trials

A wonderful couple who love the Lord Jesus came to Arrowhead Springs to attend a seminar. We sat together at the breakfast table, along with Danny, their thirteen-year-old son. He was a radiant young man who joined us in rejoicing and praising the Lord.

Following the meal, the adults moved on to the meetings. During one of the sessions, word came that Danny had been injured while roller-blading down one of the slopes on campus. His parents immediately rushed to his side.

When the ambulance arrived at the hospital, the doctors discovered that Danny had severed his spinal cord. Several hours later, he died.

You can imagine the grief, shock, and heartache his family experienced. But as the hours and days passed, Danny's parents and two older sisters believed that God was in control. This experience drew them closer to each other and the Lord.

Heartache, sorrow, and tragedy touch all our lives. Many times we cannot understand why things happen to us. The pain is so deep that it threatens to engulf us. But we can hang on to God's assurance that the Lord is with us and we will not be shaken (see Ps 16:8).

Although I have never lost a child to death, I have lived through other devastating experiences. I can say without hesitation that Christ is sufficient for any trial. He gives comfort and joy no matter how deeply you hurt. The trial will not shake you.

27 – Beyond Our Highest Hopes

Often I am asked, "Are you surprised at what God is doing through the ministry of Campus Crusade for Christ around the world?" My answer? "No, because God says in Ephesians 3:20 that He will do more in and through us than we could ever hope for."

For example, in 1946 I began to pray for the Soviet Union. The years passed. Then in 1978 at the height of the Cold War, I was invited by the government at the request of the church to tour eight cities where I spoke eighteen times. Many people indicated a response to the gospel.

Years later, we were able to arrange a premiere showing of the *JESUS* film in Moscow. Nine of the eleven government ministers and other top leaders came to the event. Following the showing, the Minister of Education asked Paul Eshelman, director of our JESUS Film Project, if we would give a videotape to 135,000 Soviet schools. We agreed. Consequently, God opened the doors to train thousands of teachers in the truths of God's Word who then have trained thousands more to reach millions of students with the gospel—all at government expense.

There is nothing too big for us to attempt for the glory of God. If our hearts and motives are pure and what we do is faithful to the Word of God, He hears and will do more than we ask or even dare to hope to accomplish.

28 – Only Through Faith

Have you ever been impressed to do something for the Lord that other people called impossible? In the '60s, I attended a Billy Graham crusade in Minneapolis. As Billy spoke, I felt God wanted Campus Crusade to call a gathering of 100,000 people for training in discipleship and evangelism. After the service, I shared the idea with Dr. Akbar Haqq, one of Billy's associate evangelists. "You must tell Billy," he said. When I did, Billy said, "I want to help."

But when I brought up the idea to the Campus Crusade staff leadership, many were afraid it would turn into a disastrous event. Could I have misread what God wanted us to do? We agreed to pray and fast about the event for several weeks. During that time, God continued to give me faith and expectancy. When we met again, the majority of staff leaders agreed to be part of the project. We knelt and dedicated our plan to God.

Faith is the basis of our Christian life. Not faith in myself, not faith in routines or programs, but faith in the Almighty Ruler of heaven and earth. When we have faith, anything is possible (see Mk 9:23).

Did God honor the faith we had for such an ambitious training program? Yes. It became the biggest event of its kind to that date. Eighty-five thousand people attended the week's training and 200,000 came for the day of praise and worship led by Billy Graham and other well-known Christians. All because God chooses to do the impossible through us.

29 – A Father's Good Gifts

Iremember times when my sons would say, "Daddy, we love you and want to please you." I would tell them, "I love you, too. I appreciate your offer to do anything I want you to do. Your expression of love is the greatest gift you can give me." Then I would put my arms around them and give them big hugs. Their love made me more sensitive about demonstrating my love to them.

Is God any less loving and concerned about His children? Of course not. He has proven over and over again that He is a loving God worthy of our trust.

As my heavenly Father, He has the wisdom and power to do for me far more than any human parent could ever do for his children. He protects, teaches, comforts, and talks to me. He goes with me through hard times and is there during my joyful experiences.

As parents, we are imperfect. We lose our temper, forget to do what we said we would do, are insensitive at times to our children's hurts and pain. Our discipline is inconsistent. But God is the perfect Father. He knows exactly what we need and want. Matthew 7:11 says that God will give good gifts to those who ask Him. Right now, He is waiting for you to ask so He can give you your heart's desire.

30 – Guardian Angels

When my grandson, Christopher, was five years old, he asked me in a serious voice, "Grandfather, are you ever afraid?"

I answered, "Christopher, there's nothing to be afraid of."

"But I'm afraid of the dark, and I'm afraid of being alone," he insisted.

I pulled him close. "Oh, but we don't have to be afraid. Whenever you feel afraid, remember that God takes care of you. He loves you more than your father does. God has given an angel instructions to guard you and report everything that happens to Him. Wherever you go and whatever you do, that angel will help you."

That promise comes from Matthew 18:10. God has a special regard for His children. The Bible calls children gifts (see Ps 127:3-5) and grandchildren a blessing (see Prv 17:6). When the disciples tried to send the children away, Jesus welcomed them with open arms.

But in this harsh, hurtful world, it can be difficult to trust God with the lives of our children. When we send them off to school or see the dangers they face, we want to protect them. When the world tries to lure them into unholy lifestyles, we want to shield them. But we cannot be there every moment.

But we can be assured that our children are always on God's mind. Their angels have constant access to God's throne. Our prayers are an ever-present way to bring them God's help and protection.

31 – God's Deepest Secrets

We all like to share in good secrets: hearing about a friend's future promotion; buying a gift for a loved one; planning a surprise party. Then comes the moment that the secret is revealed. What joy!

God has wonderful secrets to share with us. But how do we find these blessings? Through the wisdom of the Holy Spirit who will show us God's innermost thoughts (see 1 Cor 2:9,10).

But perhaps you wonder how you can receive the Holy Spirit's wisdom. As Christians, the Holy Spirit already dwells within us. It is like this. When you purchase a mechanical item that runs on battery power, frequently the notice "Batteries Not Included" is printed on the box. Unlike these items, the Holy Spirit—our source of wisdom and power for living—is "included" when you received Jesus Christ as your Savior. At that moment, the Holy Spirit gave you spiritual life. Therefore, you do not need to invite the Holy Spirit to come into your life.

When we by faith ask to be filled with the Holy Spirit, He empowers us, guides us, comforts us, gives us joy and discernment, bears spiritual fruit through us, and gives us spiritual gifts to build up the church. He also helps us understand the mysteries of God.

Walk in the power of the Holy Spirit, and He will show you wonderful things.

32 – Not Ashamed

When I was a young Christian, I was invited to a prestigious meeting in Washington, D.C., where Dr. Charles Malik, once president of the General Assembly of the United Nations, was speaking. Present were some of the most distinguished leaders in our nation and from other countries.

During his remarks, Dr. Malik emphasized his conviction that there were no human solutions to the problems that face mankind. Only Jesus Christ could help us as individuals and nations.

It impressed me that one of the world's leading statesmen would speak so boldly of his faith in Christ. I had heard others—politicians, statesmen, scholars—speak of faith in God, the Bible, and the church in general terms, but few ever spoke of their faith in the Lord Jesus Christ.

Following the meeting, I introduced myself to Dr. Malik and expressed my appreciation for his courage in speaking out so boldly for Christ. I will never forget his response. "I am sobered by the words of my Lord," he said. "'Anyone who is ashamed of me and my message in these days of unbelief and sin, I, the Messiah, will be ashamed of him when I return in the glory of my Father'" (Mk 8:38, TLB).

This axiom is true: Actions speak louder than words. If we are truly unashamed of our Savior, we will look for every opportunity to share the good news of His great love and let others know how much Jesus has done for us.

33 – Perfect Power

Along with John 3:16, Acts 3:16 is another of the great "3:16" verses of the Bible. It contains a truth that you and I need every day of our lives—that Jesus' name has all power. While on earth, Jesus taught that He had "all authority in heaven and earth" (Mt 28:18, TLB). If we exercise faith in the wonderful name of Jesus—faith that is a gift from God—we can see healing, both physical and spiritual.

I have seen the unlimited power of Jesus' name illustrated in miraculous ways in the ministry of Campus Crusade for Christ. One is the *JESUS* film, which has been used by God to introduce millions of men, women, and children to Christ in most countries of the world.

For example, *JESUS* film teams are showing the film in India. In one year, 3.4 million people viewed it. Of those, 54,567 individuals indicated salvation decisions. In Burma, communist rebels asked a film team to show *JESUS* in their camps. In Uganda, a Muslim leader became a Christian and asked that *JESUS* be shown in his mosque.

Jesus' name has perfect power to help us live righteously, tell others about Jesus, and heal us physically and spiritually. Ask God to give you faith to help heal others spiritually by introducing them to Jesus Christ. Tell them how God can forgive their sins and make something beautiful of their lives.

34 – Call on the Lord

One day a man was touring an English factory which produced the finest stationery. When he asked what the paper was made from, the guide showed him a huge pile of old rags. "The rag content determines the quality of the paper," the guide informed him. The man could not believe fine paper could be made from old rags.

Six weeks later, he received a package of paper with his initials embossed on each page. On the first page was written, "Dirty Rags Transformed."

That story is like how God transforms our lives from dirty rags of sin to pure holiness when we call on His name. I have been privileged to counsel thousands of people about their spiritual needs. Helping people see their desperate plight outside faith in Jesus Christ is sometimes difficult. No matter what their background, each person needs to recognize that he or she is lost without Christ.

Yet over the years, I have heard many thousands come to the place where they do indeed "call upon the name of the Lord" (Rom 10:13). Their new birth always gives me the greatest joy!

God does not say that we might be saved if we call on His name. He promises that we will be saved. If you help your loved one, neighbor, friend, or even a stranger become aware of God's provision for salvation, you have come a long way toward bringing that person to Christ.

35 – The Power of Praise

It is easy to praise God when life is going great. But praise means so much more when it is given during difficult times—when we are in sorrow, suffering pain, experiencing loneliness, or in the midst of stressful circumstances.

Praise, an expression of our confidence in God's faithfulness, releases His supernatural resources on our behalf. That is what I experienced one day. I was tired, and I felt like the challenges before me were overwhelming.

Then the Lord reminded me of something He had been teaching me over a period of time—the power of praise. I felt impressed to read Psalm 145. Although I did not feel like it, I began praising God. Before long, my weary, cold heart awakened to the presence of God, and I found myself praising Him out of my innermost being.

In Hebrews 13:15,16, God promises that our sacrificial praise will delight Him. When we please Him, He gives us power to rise above our circumstances. Then we experience the supernatural power of praise. We can say with the psalmist, "I will praise you, my God and King, and bless your name each day and forever" (Ps 145:1, TLB). And He will fulfill "the desires of those who reverence and trust Him" (Ps 145:19, TLB).

I encourage you to read through Psalm 145 and praise our heavenly Father—whether you feel like it or not. Such sacrifices of praise will result in special blessings.

36 – Power Over Nations

When President Gorbachev was riding the crest of popularity in the Soviet Union, Dan Peterson was our Russian representative. One day he called Vonette and me concerning a great burden he had on his heart. He urged us to organize a twenty-four-hour, thirty-day prayer vigil for the liberation of the Soviet Union.

At the time, Vonette was chairman of the Intercessory Committee of the Lausanne Movement. With the approval of the leaders in the Russian church, a plan went out to millions of Christians to unite in prayer, asking God to free the Russian people and allow them to publicly serve and worship God.

For thirty days, Christians all over the world prayed. Then the first working day following the vigil, President Gorbachev announced *glasnost* and *perestroika*. That was the beginning of great religious freedom for a nation of 300 million people.

I marvel at the promises in Revelation 2:26-28 made to the overcomer, the one who keeps on doing things to please God. He is promised power over nations!

As I ponder this verse, I see the key to the entire Christian life—"who to the very end keeps on doing things that please me." When we endure for Christ, God gives us victory over Satan, temptation, and even the forces that rule nations. That is why I believe that our prayers influence world events. What world event would you like to influence through prayer today?

37 – The Influence of Meekness

Not long ago, newspapers across America carried a heartwarming article, "The Most Powerful Man in Washington Resigns" by columnist Cal Thomas. He wrote of a remarkable man, Dr. Richard Halverson, Chaplain of the U.S. Senate for the past fifteen years. He opened every Senate session with prayer and was involved in the lives of the one hundred senators, their wives, and children. Cal Thomas described how he had seen the giants of Congress come and go, yet he had never met a man with more power than Dr. Halverson.

Dr. Halverson has been a beloved friend of mine for more than fifty years. He is one of the meekest men I have ever known. I was present in 1947 when God transformed him from a fruitless minister into a vibrant witness for Christ. His spiritual wisdom eventually thrust him into the role of a world statesman for Christ.

True meekness does not imply spinelessness. Instead, genuine meekness faces injuries, insults, abuse, and persecution with patience. Meekness is best displayed in the actions of believers who allow God to be their defense. This is patience under extreme difficulties or humility under fire and when one hardly notices when others make mistakes.

Matthew 11:29 records our Lord's meekness: "Take My yoke upon you, and learn from Me, for I am gentle and humble in heart" (NASB). Like Jesus, the meek remain calm and peaceful during confusion and chaos. That is why the meek will inherit the earth (see Mt 5:5).

38 – The Blessings of Mercy

A few years ago, I had the privilege of attending the annual Presidential Prayer Breakfast in Washington, D.C. Leaders from across America were present.

The speaker was Mother Teresa. As she walked to the podium, she looked tiny and frail. She wore her usual blue-and-white habit, an old gray sweater, and sandals. She spoke out with love and compassion about the unborn babies who were being murdered in our country through abortion. She pleaded with these world leaders to consider how precious God considers these little lives.

Although she is no longer on this earth, Mother Teresa is still a shining example of mercy. She never asked for material possessions nor demanded rights for herself. Instead, she reached into the gutter of Calcutta and loved those the world calls unlovable.

Like Mother Teresa, we can accomplish more by showing mercy to others than through almost any other act. God showed incomprehensible mercy by giving His Son to die in our place. When we show mercy to the poor, destitute, and the guilty, we show God's character. How important it is that we trust Him to make us more compassionate.

The promise given in Matthew 5:7 is clear: The merciful will obtain blessing and happiness, and more mercy from God. When we do something to glorify God, like giving a cup of cold water in His name, He considers that act as a deed of mercy done to Him—and rewards us accordingly.

39 – The Pure in Heart

When I first met Glen Jones, he was Executive Assistant to the Chairman of the Joint Chiefs of Staff. He flew the fastest planes and had a brilliant military career ahead of him. In fact, he was on the verge of becoming a general in the Air Force. Then he decided to dedicate himself to full-time Christian ministry. That is when he joined our staff.

Glen was one of the few people I have ever met who had a pure heart. I never heard him criticize anyone. His heart was full of positive thoughts.

When he was at the prime of his life, he was struck with terminal cancer. I remember sitting in a hospital room with him and his precious wife Barbara. They did not ask, "Why me, God?" Instead, they firmly said, "Whatever God wants, we want."

People with a pure heart walk humbly before God and men. They live joyful, radiant, supernatural lives for the glory of God. The pure in heart also see God because He reveals Himself to those who obey Him (see Mt 5:8). The pure in heart are the first to listen and obey.

If God seems impersonal, far off, and unreachable, examine your heart to see if you are harboring anything impure that quenches the Spirit. Check to see if sin is short-circuiting His communication with you. Then ask God to give you a pure heart. Out of your heart will spring happiness.

40 – The Overcoming Church

Through the ages, men have tried to destroy the Church, but it keeps growing worldwide at a tremendous rate. Enemies have counted the Church out, without success. Rejoice! None of the enemy's plots will ever overcome God's Church.

For 73 years, the government of the Soviet Union persecuted believers. Thousands lost their lives in forced labor camps and other difficult circumstances. Then at the height of the Cold War in 1978, Russian officials invited me to speak in their country. During a time when Westerners had little contact with the Soviet people, I spoke twenty times in eighteen Russian cities. I witnessed firsthand the vitality of the persecuted Soviet Church.

Later, God worked a miracle to bring down the Iron Curtain. The Russian Church came alive! As I write, one of the most vigorous demonstrations of the Holy Spirit at work is taking place among the Church in various republics of the former Soviet Union!

No matter how weak the Church may seem, God promises that "all the powers of hell shall not prevail against it" (Mt 16:18). Yet sometimes we see human frailties in the Church and momentarily forget its great strengths: the Word of God; believers fully committed to the Lord; genuine worship of our heavenly Father. In hard times, we can be sure that the Church is God's instrument. We can make it a rallying place for believers, a powerhouse of prayer, and a training school for sharing our faith.

First International Year

41 – Power to Witness

I once saw in a magazine a picture of the devastation produced by a Midwestern tornado. In the center of the picture was a telephone pole with a straw driven through it. How could a flimsy straw be thrust through a rugged, seasoned telephone pole? Because the straw was empowered by the awesome force of the tornado.

That is how the Holy Spirit works in our lives. Colossians 1:28 says that we are to tell everyone who will listen about Christ. When we obey in God's power, He produces the fruit.

For example, one of my dear friends who is a great Christian scholar told me that he was not a joyful Christian and seldom witnessed for Christ. I shared with him some of the truths about how to witness in the power of the Holy Spirit. God touched his life. He came back bubbling with joy from an afternoon of sharing Christ. He described how he had talked to two young college students about Christ. Christ had become more real to him than he had ever experienced.

To become a powerful witness, realize that you are filled with the Holy Spirit the same way you became a Christian—by faith. (Compare Ephesians 2:8 with Colossians 2:6.) Ask God to give you the power to tell everyone you meet about His love and forgiveness. Then faithfully talk about our Lord and leave the results to God. He will do more with your witness than you can imagine!

42 – Blessings of Faith

Mary, the mother of Jesus, is one of the most remarkable women in history. She believed God would do what He said even when the facts seemed impossible. Imagine what she must have faced. No one before her had experienced such an unusual pregnancy. How could she explain it to others? What would God expect her to do? How would it change her life?

No doubt Mary was chosen to be the mother of Jesus because of the faith God knew she possessed. God honored her faith and gave her the highest privilege any mother could have—raising God's only Son. He also knew that she would be faithful to the end, throughout Christ's ministry, death, and resurrection. Nothing could shake her belief that God would do what He said He would do.

We can also claim blessing for our faith. If we truly believe that God will do what He says, the wonderful blessings He promises will be ours. And that applies to every area of our lives—spiritual, physical, and material.

What is your greatest need today? If you are a housewife and mother, it may be for patience. If you are a business or professional person, it may be for wisdom. If you are a student, it may be for persistence.

None of us can experience a situation in which God cannot work for our good. When we fully trust Him, He blesses us with wonderful things that we do not expect or imagine.

43 – Sowing Seed

If you ask any farmer, he will agree with this principle: If we sow our best seed in the most fertile soil, we can expect an abundant return. The axiom of abundant return is simple. The crop is always more plentiful than its seed.

A wheat, flax, and sunflower farmer in North Dakota, plants a given amount of seed each season for a desire yield per acre. From one-and-one-half bushels of wheat, he expects to harvest up to forty bushels. Under favorable growing conditions, two-thirds bushel of flax will produce about twenty bushels, and one-eighth bushel or four pounds of sunflower seed will return up to 1,500 pounds.

A single redwood tree can reproduce itself millions of times during its lifetime. A grape seedling is capable of branching into a prolific vine filled with luscious fruit. One peach pit will sprout into a tree laden with delicious produce.

I have the privilege of working with hundreds of dedicated, Christian laymen who have discovered the law of abundant return. Again and again they have seen the truth of God's promise in Isaiah 55:10,11. The more they sow God's Word, the more they see fruit in changed lives.

Today the world is waiting for answers to unsolvable problems. People are looking for someone who can deliver them from sin's poison. We have the most powerful antidote ever known—God's Word. Share His life-giving message with everyone you meet.

44 – Overflowing Generosity

The Sea of Galilee is a harp-shaped lake in the Jordan Valley. It is fed by the Jordan River, which exits through a fertile valley at the southern tip of the lake. The region produces abundant crops of grain, fruits, and vegetables. Wild flowers and oleanders fringe the shoreline.

In contrast, the Dead Sea—just sixty-five miles downstream—is a harsh, saline body of water. Its freshwater source is also the Jordan River. But unlike the Sea of Galilee, the Dead Sea has no outlet. As a result, the water is bitter to taste and nauseous to smell. The surrounding landscape is a barren chaos of crags and wadis. The sea is so salty and saturated with minerals that a person can float on his back and read a newspaper. I did this once when I visited the area.

Two bodies of water. One sweet and overflowing; the other bitter and lifeless. One receives and gives; the other receives and hoards.

Many Christians resemble these lakes. Some give generously to God's work and God blesses them. Others hang on to what God has entrusted to them. They build larger estates and bank accounts. They miss so much joy because, like the Dead Sea, they have no outlet for giving to others.

To experience the joy of giving, invest generously in His work. When you do, you will reap the blessings God has in store for those who give generously (see Prv 22:9).

45 – The Confiscated Bibles

In Isaiah 59:21, we read that God's Word will not depart from our children. In 2 Timothy 1:1-10, we learn about Timothy who was trained in the Word by his mother and grandmother, which resulted in much fruit in this young man's life. God's Word will not return void, as the following story shows.

In the 1930s, Stalin ordered a purge of all Bibles. In Stavropol, Russia, thousands of Bibles were confiscated.

Recently, the CoMission, an organization committed to evangelizing the former Soviet Union, sent a team to Stavropol. But their shipment of Bibles did not arrive in time. Then someone mentioned a warehouse outside of town where those confiscated Bibles had been stored since Stalin's day.

After much prayer by the team, one member asked city officials if the Bibles could be distributed to the people of Stavropol. The answer was "Yes!"

The next day, the team returned with a truck and several Russians to help load the Bibles. One was a skeptical collegian only interested in the wages. As the workers loaded the Bibles, the young man disappeared. Soon they found him in a corner of the warehouse, weeping. While loading the shipment, he had quietly taken a Bible. Opening the cover, he found his grandmother's signature! Out of thousands of Bibles, he had taken the one belonging to his grandmother.

That faithful woman had probably prayed for him for years. Today, her grandson is studying the very Bible she found so dear.

46 – Proof of Eternal Life

A ll Scripture is given to us for a purpose—to help us share Christ's message with unbelievers. That is why John wrote his Gospel, so that first we might believe, and then that we might share the good news with all who will listen. John's arguments are irrefutable, framed after the strictest rules of evidence, written to convince those who look at the proof that they can have eternal life (see Jn 20:31).

But this is not just the message of John's Gospel; it is also the core of the New Testament.

Recently, Chaplain Thaddeus Horbowy of the Federal Bureau of Prisons Federal Deportation Center called our ministry to share an exciting story. He works with foreign inmates scheduled to be deported to their countries. Chaplain Horbowy needed materials in foreign languages to reach these detainees with Christ's message.

He received copies of the *JESUS* video in Arabic, Polish, Russian, French, German, Vietnamese, Chinese, Korean, and Swahili. The *JESUS* video is taken almost word for word from the Gospel of Luke.

The chaplain called a few weeks later. "Thank you! Thank you! Our Vietnamese detainees are eagerly signing up to see the video you sent us; Jewish detainees are watching the video in Russian; and others are watching in Arabic.… It makes such a difference when they are able to hear the message of Christ in their own language."

What a message we have to share! What responses we will see!

47 – The Most Important Moment

Many years ago, Martin Luther mused, "I cannot think what we shall find to do in heaven. No change, no work, no eating, no drinking, nothing to do."

"Yes," responded a friend, "Lord, show us the Father, and it sufficeth us."

"Why, of course," Luther said, "that sight will give us quite enough to do."

We have an appointment that is more important than fame and fortune, more precious than any wealth we may obtain, superior than any honor we can receive now. The greatest moment of our lives will be when we enter the glorious presence of our loving Lord!

Some years ago, my 93-year-old father went to be with the Lord, and a year later, my precious mother joined him. I still miss them, and there is a soft place in my heart for them. But I believe the most important moment of their lives was when they breathed their last breath on earth.

I know they are now rejoicing in the presence of our wonderful God and Savior. One day I shall join them, along with my brothers and sisters and multitudes of loved ones and friends. We will spend eternity with Jesus (see Jn 14:3).

We do not need to know exactly what heaven will be like. We only need to know who will be there—our Lord Jesus Christ and our heavenly Father. As Luther realized, we will worship God face to face throughout the endless ages of eternity.

48 – Resurrection Proof

As a young skeptic, I had difficulty believing in the resurrection because I did not believe in the supernatural. But when I became aware of the uniqueness of Jesus and the perfect life He lived, I reconsidered His resurrection. I set out to discover if His tomb could have been empty for any other reason than His resurrection. In my research, I learned that there are three theories used to explain away the empty tomb.

First, Jesus fainted from a loss of blood on the cross. Later He recovered in the coolness of the tomb. This is called the "swoon theory." Second, Jesus' body was stolen by His enemies. Third, His body was taken by His disciples.

Experience and logic forced me to discount all three theories. First, in His weakened condition, Jesus could not have moved the stone or escaped from the guards. Second, Jesus' enemies had no reason to steal His body. Even if they took it, surely they would have produced it to discount resurrection claims. Third, the disciples who deserted Jesus at His crucifixion spent the rest of their lives telling others—even at the cost of their lives—that Jesus was alive. Would they be willing to die as martyrs while propagating a lie?

In John 11:25, Jesus claimed that He could raise the dead. With His resurrection, He proved that He can give life after death. Therefore, the resurrection assures us that He will give us life after death.

49 – Avoiding Problems

After he was given his assignment, a newly appointed director of affairs for our ministry came to me for counsel. "What are the biggest problems I'll encounter in my new area of responsibility?"

"The first of three major ones you may face," I responded, "is pride, the problem that caused Satan to seek a place of authority over God and resulted in his expulsion from heaven. Since creation, man's greatest problem has been pride.

"Your second problem will be materialism—the desire to accumulate wealth, to live the good life, to keep up with the Joneses.

"The third problem will be the temptation to be immoral. In marriage, sex is a God-given privilege. But outside marriage, sex grieves the Holy Spirit and results in God's discipline.

"I encourage you to start by getting to know God better. Then be faithful to your wife and love her as God loves the church (see Eph 5:25). Keep yourself humble by living a Spirit-filled life in God's power. Seek the simple. Be motivated by the love of God for the souls of men, rather than for the good things of this world."

This is my message to all Christian leaders and those who want to live a godly life. Our faith is a gift from God, measured by Him. As we get to know Him better, He enables us to live a good life, resist temptation, and build up His kingdom.

50 – A Wonderful Friendship

Let me tell you about my best friend. He is my Lord, my Savior, my Master, and King. I talk to Him about everything. I share my needs with Him, my heartaches, my sorrows, and disappointments. I ask Him to give me resolution for my problems and help with conflicts.

He gives me wisdom and counsel; He comforts me and protects me. He encourages, inspires, motivates, and enlightens me. As you have probably guessed, Jesus Christ is my best friend.

You and I do not always prove faithful, but the Lord Jesus Christ stays right beside us. As close friends, Christians participate with Christ in several ways:

First, in His trials and sufferings, for we are subjected to trials similar to His: "But rejoice, inasmuch as ye are partakers of Christ's sufferings" (1 Pt 4:13, KJV).

Second, in His feelings and views: "You have the Spirit of God living in you" (Rom 8:9, TLB).

Third, in the inheritance and glory which awaits Him: "And if children, then heirs; heirs of God, and joint-heirs with Christ" (Rom 8:17, KJV).

Fourth, in His future triumph: "Ye which have followed me, in the regeneration when the Son of man shall sit in the throne of his glory, ye also shall sit upon twelve thrones, judging the twelve tribes of Israel" (Mt 19:28, KJV).

Are you not glad for that kind of friendship? We can depend on the faithfulness of God who invited us into this fellowship with His Son.

51 – We Are Comforters

Recently, I flew from Atlanta to Dallas for a conference on evangelism. I was seated beside a pro football player who was about 6'6" tall and 250 pounds. As we chatted about spiritual matters, he said, "I need your help. My father-in-law passed away a week ago. My wife and mother-in-law are devastated with grief. What can I say to comfort them?"

Since I, too, have experienced the heartache of losing loved ones, including my own mother and father, I could empathize with his pain. I explained, "Before you can help your family, you need to let God help you. He is the source of true comfort."

As I read through the Four Spiritual Laws with him, he asked Christ to be the Savior and Lord of his life. As we talked, he expressed how excited he was about telling his wife and mother-in-law that they, too, could know the love, grace, and comfort of God through Jesus Christ.

God never comforts His children solely for their own ends or just so they will feel better. Every experience in life is given through the love of our Lord. He wants us to trust Him to turn our hardships and trials into sympathy and encouragement that we can pass on to our friends, loved ones, and people we meet "this same help and comfort" (2 Cor 1:3,4, TLB).

As God blesses us, He expects us to pass the blessing on to others.

52 – Assured Peace and Victory

Perhaps you have felt the same as Don and Ann did. With all their hearts they wanted to please the Lord. They worked at being victorious Christians. They diligently kept their quiet times and memorized Scripture, and faithfully attended church. They did everything right. But they said, "Although we've claimed the fullness of the Holy Spirit by faith and tried to identify ourselves with Christ, we just don't seem to be enjoying the Christian life. There's something missing."

"In Philippians 4," I told them, "you will find a surefire spiritual formula for victory in the Christian life. Just allow the Holy Spirit to make this passage a reality to you and apply it as He enables you." Then I gave them these points that lead to God's supernatural peace:

1. As an act of your will, decide that you are going to be full of the joy of the Lord. You are the one who decides whether you are going to rejoice or be discouraged and sad.

2. Demonstrate an unselfish, considerate attitude.

3. Remember that the Lord can come at any moment, so be prepared.

4. Do not worry about anything.

5. Pray about everything.

6. Thank Him in faith for His answers.

Practicing these steps leads to one of the most priceless experience we can know—the supernatural peace of God. It cannot be purchased or acquired any other way. These six steps also lead to assured victory in our lives.

53 – True Revival

What is revival? Today churches declare "revival" if they have a few exciting services. But revival is much more than that. Spiritual renewal is something that only God can produce in us. Ephesians 3:20 tells us that He will use His mighty power to work in us in ways beyond our highest prayers, desires, and hopes.

What are some characteristics of revival?

1. Revival is a sovereign act of God. The Holy Spirit is the One who orchestrates revival.

2. Revival is a divine visitation. Spiritual renewal is God's idea; believers simply respond to His work.

3. Revival is a time of personal humiliation, forgiveness, and restoration in the Holy Spirit.

4. During revival, preaching is fearless under the anointing of the Holy Spirit.

5. The presence of the Holy Spirit is powerful. People literally fall down on their faces before God.

6. Revival changes communities and nations. During the Welsh revival, crime disappeared; judges had no cases to try. In the past, revival has shaped the moral direction of America.

We desperately need revival today. But we do not need to wait for a sovereign act of God to bring revival. Our task is to surrender to the lordship of Christ and the control of the Holy Spirit, fast and pray, and obey God's Word. Meeting these conditions, we can expect the Holy Spirit to do far more than we dare ask or dream!

54 – Proof of His Love

When Vonette and I disciplined Zac and Brad, we did it in love, not anger. When one of our sons disobeyed us, we would first explain why we were punishing him. Then we would follow through with the appropriate discipline. When it was all over, we would hug him and emphasize that we disciplined him because we loved him.

One day Zac came home from kindergarten with a puzzled look on his face. With a serious tone, he announced, "I don't think many of the children at school have parents who love them like you love me."

Mystified, Vonette asked, "Why do you say that, honey?"

"Because they are so disobedient," he said confidently.

Even at his young age, Zac understood that a part of love is correction. This is true of our relationship with God, too. He disciplines us because He loves us. He knows how important it is for us to live by the boundaries He has set up in His Word. He shows His loving care when He makes us accountable for our sins. And sometimes that hurts!

So whenever you face a hurtful situation, ask yourself, "Is there something in my life that displeases God? Is He trying to turn me from some temptation?" If the answer is yes, thank Him for being a caring Father who wants the best for His children. Then confess any sin He brings to your mind and commit yourself to walking in His Spirit once again.

55 – The Will of God

I have not always cared about the will of God. During my childhood in Coweta, Oklahoma, my mother was a Christian but my father was not. As I grew up, I tried to take on the "macho" image of my father, considering Christianity for women and children but not for me. I was determined that in spite of my shy nature, I would be strong and self-reliant and accomplish anything I set out to accomplish.

I went away to college determined to become student body president, editor of the yearbook, and named to Who's Who in American Colleges and Universities. In four years, I accomplished each objective.

When I moved to California, I had no clue that God had a far better plan for me. I was a "happy pagan"—an agnostic, who did not know if God existed and really did not care.

I rented an apartment from a charming elderly couple in Holly wood and began pouring my life into building a new fancy-foods enterprise, Bright's California Confections. God used this dear couple to draw me to Himself. I may have made a fortune with my business, achieved much in the eyes of the world, but what would I have gained? Nothing. Instead, I have lived a life of adventure and by His grace, have impacted millions of people. As 1 John 2:17 says, "The world and its desires pass away, but the man who does the will of God lives forever" (NIV).

Are you living in the will of God? It is the greatest way to experience peace and eternal fruit.

56 – Work for the Lord

In 1951, I was in my senior year at Fuller Theological Seminary. For two exciting years, I had been married to my hometown sweetheart, the former Vonette Zachary. Vonette had accepted a teaching position in the Los Angeles school system, and we were living a busy and eventful life.

In addition to regular meetings at church, I led a deputation group of more than one hundred dedicated young college-age men and women who wanted to serve the Lord Jesus Christ. We covered approximately thirty assignments each month, visiting local jails and hospitals, and skid-row missions. I soon discovered that we had to wait our turn because so many other churches were covering these areas of service.

One day it occurred to me that there were no waiting lines to reach college students or the city's top executives. Here were the neglected leaders of our world, both today's and tomorrow's. This began a focus that eventually led to the ministry of Campus Crusade on college campuses and in communities where we saw many talented young men and women turn their lives over to Christ.

Since then, the truth of 1 Corinthians 15:58 has become even clearer to me. "Always give yourselves fully to the work of the Lord, because you know that your labor in the Lord is not in vain" (NIV). The Lord's leading in His work leads to abundant fruitfulness. As we look to Him for guidance and strength, He will guide us into the areas He has prepared for us.

57 – Finding Happiness

What does material success mean to you? When I was first entering business, I wanted to have all the possessions associated with wealth as well as a growing bank account. I believed that if I worked hard, I could accumulate all the things I desired.

About that time, there were a number of successful businessmen in the church I attended, Hollywood Presbyterian, including a prominent builder who often invited small groups of young people into his home for picnics and swimming.

During one of these popular events, we asked him what it was like to be so successful. His answer startled me. "Material success is not where you find happiness," he stated firmly. "There are rich people all over this city who are the most miserable people you'll ever meet. Knowing and serving Jesus Christ is what's important. He is the only way to find happiness."

This godly man was following Christ's teachings in Luke 12. After showing how fleeting material needs are, He says, "For the pagan world runs after all such things, and your Father knows that you need them. But seek his kingdom, and these things will be given to you as well" (vv. 30,31, NIV).

My godly mother exemplified this principle. Now I was meeting sharp young adults and successful men and women who were living what my mother had lived. Through their examples, I learned that seeking God's kingdom rather than material possessions leads to true happiness.

58 – All-Important Question

Before I was a believer, I was greatly impressed with the eloquence of pastor Dr. Louis Evans. He presented Jesus Christ in a way I had never known before, so I began an in-depth study of the life of Jesus. The more I read, the more I became convinced that He is truly the Son of God.

On a Sunday in 1945, Dr. Henrietta Mears, director of Christian education at Hollywood Presbyterian Church, described Paul's conversion on the Damascus road. She came to the part where Paul asked, "Who are You, Lord, and what will You have me do?" She said, "This is one of the most important questions you can ask God today." She challenged us to go home, get on our knees, and ask God that all-important question.

That night, I knelt beside my bed and asked that question. In a sense, that was my prayer for salvation. It wasn't theologically sound, but the Lord knew my heart. Though nothing dramatic or emotional happened when I prayed, I know without a doubt that Jesus came into my life. My decision did not seem very dramatic at first, but as I began to grow in my new commitment and love for the Lord, I became more aware of what a sinner I was and what a wonderful, forgiving Savior He is.

Do you know without a doubt that Jesus is in your life? If you invite Him to come into your life, He will (see Rv 3:20).

59 – The Contract

Before our commitments to the Lord, Vonette and I both held materialistic goals. Our dreams included the finest European honeymoon, a home in the fabulous Bel-Air district of Los Angeles, expensive cars, and other things. But after we decided to make Christ Lord of our lives, we began to respond to His command: "Seek first his kingdom and his righteousness" (Mt 6:33, NIV). Every day in some new and exciting way, we learned that God's will was better than our own.

One Sunday afternoon, we talked about how our trust in God had grown. We wondered what new goals we should place before Him. Vonette came up with an excellent suggestion, "Why don't we go into separate rooms and make a list of things that are important to us? Then we'll compare notes and agree on a final list."

We did just that. When we came back together, our priorities were surprisingly the same, although expressed in different words. The top priority was to live holy lives controlled and empowered by the Holy Spirit. Second was to be effective witnesses, and third to help fulfill the Great Commission (see Mt 28:18-20).

We signed our names to these lists as a formal act of commitment to Christ. This was an especially significant moment because we were doing it as a couple. We felt no particular emotion; it was simply an act of our wills.

Have you made a commitment to serve Christ unreservedly? Out of this commitment will come God's blessing and guidance in your life.

*Bill Bright with Billy Graham and Dr. Joon Gon Kim at
the Billy Graham Crusade in April 1973.*

60 – Our Boast in God

By nature I have always been a bit reserved—even shy. I have never been a particularly dramatic or highly entertaining speaker. There was a time when I dreamed of becoming a great orator. But one day a wise seminary professor admonished his class, "When you speak, do you want people to marvel at what a great speaker you are, or at what a great God you serve?"

That challenge convicted me, and ever since I have always sought to communicate as simply and directly as possible. I pray that God will speak to the hearts of the audience and that His wonderful plan will be made clear to everyone.

I say this to emphasize that neither I nor anyone can take any human credit for what God has done through Campus Crusade. It has been totally a work of God. As Psalm 44:8 says, "In God we make our boast all day long, and we will praise your name forever" (NIV).

None of us can claim a single honor for anything we have done. What we have accomplished, we have done in the power of the Holy Spirit, with His wisdom, and with the principles of Scripture. God gives us the endurance and patience. Today when I speak all over the world, it is still God who is helping me.

What have you done recently for which you can give God the credit? By praising Him we give witness of His power in our lives.

61 – Concern for America

Recently, John N. Damoose and I co-authored a book, *Red Sky in the Morning*, to encourage concerned citizens in our beloved country to join us in bringing about a moral and spiritual rebirth in America. We wrote with burning hearts and a great sense of urgency. In the book, we asked all followers of Jesus Christ to pray, fast, and work for a revival in our churches and for a mighty spiritual awakening across our land.

Our concern is great because, according to most social indicators, we as a nation are in danger of losing our soul. Our Lord's warning to individuals also applies to nations: "What will it profit a man, if he gains the whole world and forfeits his life?" (Mt 16:26, RSV). The problems facing America are severe. Solving these problems is a matter of life and death for our beloved country.

Only God can help us find solutions to this present moral crisis, the greatest our nation has ever faced. Unless He sovereignly and super-naturally intervenes, our nation shall lose its soul, and the consequences will be worse than Russia's revolution under Lenin or Stalin or Germany's under Hitler.

I encourage you to study our nation's spiritual history. I urge you to pray fervently that we will turn once again to God and turn away from the evil that ensnares us. As we all unite in prayer, we will see God's Holy Spirit do miraculous things for our country.

62 – The Greatest Mission

One of the most essential concepts in Scripture is found in the 28th chapter of Matthew. It has a deep significance to us as Christ's followers. Just before Jesus ascended into heaven, He told His disciples, "All authority in heaven and on earth has been given to me. Therefore go and make disciples of all nations, baptizing them in the name of the Father and of the Son and of the Holy Spirit, and teaching them to obey everything I have commanded you. And surely I am with you always, to the very end of the age" (Mt 28:18-20, NIV).

These instructions have been known throughout Church history as the Great Commission. In other words, Christ commissioned His disciples and all who would receive Him throughout the centuries to continue His ministry of "seeking and saving the lost" (Lk 19:10).

Our Lord has called us to share His message of eternal salvation with the entire world. It is the greatest mission in which any person can possibly participate.

Imagine! God has chosen to speak through us to a lost world, giving us the privilege of helping introduce others to His Son Jesus Christ, the living Lord and Savior! Because of the Great Commission's central place in God's eternal plan, I have committed my life to helping fulfill it in our generation. Join me in the greatest joy in life—seeing someone become a member of the family of God as he or she receives Christ as Savior and Lord.

63 – Reluctant Warriors

At various times and places throughout history, God sent special ambassadors to change the world. I think immediately of individuals like Martin Luther, John Knox, John Wesley, William Wilberforce, and George Whitefield, who bore words of passion and renewal. There were some, such as Winston Churchill, who spoke of duty, honor, and country in times of world crisis. Some like Mother Teresa of Calcutta spoke for all those who were suffering and could not speak for themselves. We see the impact of other less-known but faithful Christians through their deeds in small and inconspicuous ways.

Could any of these brave souls have avoided their calling from God? Absolutely. Could the world have continued on without them? Probably, but not nearly so well. Can our churches' moral courage and strength continue if you and I fail to live up to God's calling upon our lives? That is a question every one of us must answer.

Most believers miss the very mission that God has given them. They may be active in the church a couple days each week, but neglect the needs of those who surround them the other five days. Why do we withhold the matchless offer of salvation Christ has made available to us? Perhaps because of embarrassment, lack of knowledge, and our intimidation by the cultural hostility to Christ and His gospel. We must not be reluctant warriors, but those ready to fight the battle in spiritual armor (see Eph 6:11-20).

64 – It's in the Training

Iremember a brilliant young college student whom I had introduced to Christ. In my ignorance I was always haranguing him to witness for Jesus. I never taught him, however, how to appropriate the power of the Holy Spirit by faith or what to say when talking to nonbelievers.

One day he became very impatient. "Get off my back," he protested. "You're making life miserable. I don't want anything more to do with you. Go away; get lost!"

I was shocked and hurt. But he was absolutely right in not wanting anything to do with me. He needed help, but I was not mature enough to help him.

As a result I began to realize that many Christians loved and wanted to serve the Lord as much as I did. They just needed someone to teach them how to share their faith. Then I became less judgmental in my attitudes toward other believers.

Have you done what I did—make other believers feel guilty about their failure to witness without coming alongside to help? We need to show our friends how to discover the joy of introducing others to Christ. Or perhaps you are a person who desires to share his faith but are discouraged because you do not know how. Believers need encouragement and training, not criticism for their failures. I encourage you to find someone who is leading others to Christ and ask to be trained in sharing your faith.

65 – Our Measure of Devotion

Paul described his own selfless commitment to Christ when he wrote, "I have been crucified with Christ and I no longer live, but Christ lives in me. The life I live in the body, I live by faith in the Son of God, who loved me and gave himself for me" (Gal 2:20, NIV). In light of all God has done for us, dare we have any less devotion? The gospel of Jesus Christ is all-consuming truth or an optional theory. God's truth must completely possess each person who claims to be Christ's follower. We must have a passion for our Lord that is radical, sold-out, engaged, and fully dedicated. Anything less is potentially harmful.

Paul says, "You are not your own; you were bought at a price" (1 Cor 6:19-20, NIV). That price was Christ's own blood shed on the cross for our sins. When we stop to consider the price that Jesus paid to bring us to Himself, we should recognize that "cheap grace" and "easy believism" are a stench to our holy God. True grace should fill us with gratitude overflowing into obedience as we return that love to Him.

Commitment comes with a price tag. As true believers, we must be willing to pay the price—however great or small that may be. When we understand the value of the unlimited gift of grace, we respond with abiding faith. Only when we have died to self can we truly live for Him.

66 – World-Changers for Christ

For approximately fifty years, I have been convinced that the Great Commission of Christ as recorded in Matthew 28:18-20 will be fulfilled in our generation. There was a time not all that long ago, however, when this goal seemed overly ambitious. The logistics were simply too great. But in the last five years, that has changed. Suddenly we have the manpower, the resources, and an unprecedented window of opportunity to help reach the entire world for Christ. He calls us to serve—even to be world-changers—and He has given us His Holy Spirit to empower us to do what He has called us to do.

In my travels, I have seen abundant evidence of how the world looks to the West. Since the fall of communism, the collapse of the Berlin Wall, and the opening of Chinese markets to Western interests, America has enhanced its influence. Borders that had been closed for decades are suddenly open to us, competing for American technology and products. Political and corporate leaders are looking for new ideas and leadership principles.

Chuck Colson warns that all too often we have led the world, not to the freedom of Christ, but to the bondage of sin. We cannot let this be the only America they see!

The harvest fields are ripe. How eagerly people around the world respond to the news of Jesus Christ. Are we awakening? Let us be alert and fight the battle before us!

67 – Prayer of Confession

If you have never received Jesus Christ as your personal Savior, or if you are not sure you have, or if there is no evidence of any changes in your life since you first prayed for forgiveness, then I urge you to examine your spiritual condition carefully. You can do it now. There is nothing stopping you from asking Jesus to come into your heart, to forgive your sins, and to be the Lord of your life in all things.

God will not force Himself on us. Each of us must decide as an act of our free will to move toward God. Do not wait until you get your life in better shape. He will accept you just as you are right now. Do not wait until you better understand the person and ways of God to get things figured out in your mind. None of us understands God fully. Just come to Him in faith and pour your heart and hurts out to Him as you ask for His forgiveness and help.

Through the prophet Ezekiel, God said, "Repent, and turn from all your transgressions, so that iniquity will not be your ruin" (Ez 18:30, NKJV). Your honest, heartfelt prayer of confession will reach the very throne room of heaven and God will answer. (See Ps 91:15; Is 58:9; 65:24; Lk 11:9; Jn 15:7.)

Your prayer will be heard. Be assured that "whoever calls on the name of the Lord shall be saved" (Jl 2:32, NKJV).

68 – Lasting Legacy

On my way through Oklahoma for my December 30th wedding to my sweetheart, Vonette Zachary, I passed through the city of Okmulgee where my grandfather had lived for many years. Suddenly, I remembered that I needed to purchase gifts for the wedding party, so I stopped at a jewelry store.

Before looking for the items I wanted, I asked the owner if he would cash an out-of-state check. He shook his head. "I'm sorry, sir. That's against our policy."

As I turned to walk out of the store, he asked me if I knew anyone in the city.

"No," I replied, "my grandfather used to live here, but he's been dead for several years."

"What's his name?" the owner asked.

"Sam Bright."

"Are you the grandson of Sam Bright?"

I nodded.

"Sam Bright was the most honorable man I have ever known!" he exclaimed. "If you're anything like your grandfather, I will sell you anything in this store. And I'll take your check!"

I felt moved by his reply. My grandfather had left a legacy of integrity.

Our legacy is the most important asset we leave behind when we die. What will it say about us? Psalm 112:6 says, "The righteous shall be in everlasting remembrance" (KJV) and Proverbs 10:7 says, "The memory of the just is blessed" (KJV). Our legacy reflects how we lived and how our lives affected others. Let's strive for a lasting legacy that points to our heavenly Father.

69 – Giving by Faith

Giving by faith is a principle basic to Spirit-directed stewardship. Simply defined, giving by faith is taking God at His Word and giving generously as He provides.

The premise of this concept is threefold. First, God is the absolute source of our supply. Second, giving is based on His resources, not our own. Third, Christ is our link to God's inexhaustible riches. Paul includes these precepts in his letter to the Christians at Philippi, "My God shall supply all your need according to His riches in glory by Christ Jesus" (Phil 4:19, NKJV).

When we place our trust in people or things, we soon discover their limitations in helping us. Acknowledging God as the source of all we need gives us a clear vision of His power to provide. As we reflect on His bountiful nature, He impresses on us to give more than we could ever give through our human abilities. We depend on His riches rather than our own limited reservoir. We access these riches because of Christ's sacrifice on the cross, as joint-heirs with Him, blessed with "every spiritual blessing in the heavenly places" in Christ (Eph 1:3).

If we ever plan to do anything for Christ and His kingdom, we must do it now! Growing worldwide problems and unprecedented opportunities for Christian ministry make giving by faith a priority. When we think of the eternal destiny of billions of people, we will be motivated by a great sense of urgency!

70 – The Good Soil

An abundant harvest springs from the most fertile soil. No intelligent farmer would think of planting seed in poorly prepared soil. Rather, he prepares the soil thoroughly with the finest equipment and fertilizers. He knows that the quality of the ground and its preparation are vital.

Ideally, soil must be heavy enough to resist wind erosion, yet light enough to mix well when tilled. Good earth holds the moisture and allows the roots to penetrate the ground. Hard soil will not let the water soak in. Sandy soil dries out too quickly. Black, rich dirt which contains little sand and no alkali or clay is best.

Cultivation is crucial as well. The soil must be tilled until soft enough for planting, but not so loose that it will dry out. Tilling also rids the soil of weeds, which rob moisture and nutrients from the seedlings and prevent the sunlight from producing strong, healthy plants.

Preparing the soil of our hearts is just as vital. When our hearts are hard, we cannot produce a vibrant crop of good deeds and righteousness. And sometimes we do not cultivate the soil correctly. Many Christians experience financial problems, emotional turmoil, even physical illness because they are sowing seed in the unproductive soil of wrongdoing and unworthy enterprises.

I challenge you to sow God's Word into the soil of a humble attitude to see the best return on your investment. Reap the joy that comes with an abundant spiritual harvest (see Gal 6:8).

Bill and Vonette Bright with Corrie ten Boom

71 – A Nation Under God

More than six hundred Christian leaders, representing more than a hundred religious organizations, gathered in Orlando, Florida, on December 5–7, 1994, in response to a special call to fasting and prayer for America and the fulfillment of the Great Commission. They came together to beseech the Lord to visit us from heaven with miracle-working power so that we may once again be a "nation under God" (NIV).

It all started on July 5th when God led me to begin a forty-day fast. On my twenty-ninth day of fasting, I was reading 2 Chronicles 20-30 when God's Word spoke to my heart in an unusual way. I felt impressed by the Lord to invite several hundred influential Christians to Orlando as guests of Campus Crusade for a time of fasting and prayer. This would be strictly a time for seeking God's direction on how we, His servants, can be channels of revival for our nation and the world.

I was hoping for a Gideon's three hundred to respond. Instead, more than six hundred came.

God met with us in a supernatural way. Many remarked how they had never been a part of anything so spiritually powerful in their lives. I believe that as millions of Christians rediscover the power of fasting as recorded in 2 Chronicles 7:14, they will come alive. And out of this great move of the Spirit of God will come the revival for which we have prayed so long.

72 – God's Call to America

As I knelt before the Lord at my favorite chair in our living room, I was sobered by the conditions that the Holy Spirit had placed on His promise to send revival. These conditions seemed to match the spirit of 2 Chronicles 7:14, "If my people, who are called by my name, will humble themselves and pray and seek my face and turn from their wicked ways, then will I hear from heaven and will forgive their sin and will heal their land" (NIV).

America provides more money, technology, and manpower to help fulfill the Great Commission than all other countries combined. If the enemies of the gospel have their way, America will no longer be a great sending nation.

With 2 Chronicles 7:14 strongly in my mind, I sensed the Holy Spirit was telling me that millions of believers must seek God with all their hearts in fasting and prayer before He will intervene to save America. I was impressed by the Spirit to pray that two million believers will humble themselves by seeking God in forty-day fasts.

I challenge you to commit yourself to becoming one of the two million who fast and pray for our country. Not an appeal to emotions, revival is an act of the will. Our remaining time here on earth is very short. The Lord may come soon, or He may challenge us to do more for Him than we are now doing. Our nation needs revival. Revival starts with us.

73 – Revival Is Coming

I believe God wants to spare our nation from its moral morass, and I am confident that He is going to send a great spiritual awakening to America and the world. God is touching the hearts of many Christians across our land, as He has touched mine. He is convicting His people—persuading them of their sin and the sins of the country—in preparation for the coming revival.

In his book *The Turning Tide*, Pat Robertson says the hearts of the people are yearning for a return to the values that made America great. Yet few seem to grasp how easy it would be for God's revival fire to sweep around the world. Past revivals show just how powerful our Lord really is.

The Lord ignited the New England colonies in the mid-1700s with the powerful, soul-searching sermons of Jonathan Edwards. George Whitefield joined Edwards in this preaching, and so many sinners were converted that the course of the nation was changed. The 1904 Welsh revival spread to other continents, spanning the oceans to America where twenty million came to Christ.

During my first forty-day fast, the Holy Spirit assured me again and again that God will send a revival to America and the world when His people heed His call to turn to Him (see 2 Chr 7:14). I am confident that this awakening will result in the greatest spiritual harvest in history, and that the Great Commission will be fulfilled in our generation.

74 – Stepping Out in Faith

If I can learn how to share my faith, so can you. I remember my first witnessing experience. I was scared to death. It is as clear as though it happened just this morning.

Bob was an outstanding businessman who had just begun attending our church. As I became acquainted with him, I felt that the Lord wanted me to talk with Bob about his salvation. But I had no idea what to say.

I argued that someone more qualified would be better to approach him. But I could not shake the uncomfortable feeling that God wanted me to be the one. I was reminded of Matthew 4:19, "Follow me, and I will make you fishers of men," (KJV). I realized it was my responsibility to simply obey Him. His responsibility was to do the inner work of changing human hearts.

So with a dry mouth and pounding heart, I spoke with Bob about inviting Jesus Christ into his life. As we sat in his car, half a block from the church, I showed him some Scriptures about man's need for God. To my amazement Bob prayed with me right then, asking the Lord Jesus to forgive him of his sin and to come into his life.

Shortly after, he resigned his position and entered seminary. He has been a minister for more than thirty-five years now, helping others trust Christ and grow in their walks with Him. You, too, can experience this joy as you share your faith with others.

75 – The Power of Simplicity

I encourage you to find a simple way of sharing your faith. I am convinced that one of the reasons for the phenomenal effectiveness we see in the ministry of such men as Dwight L. Moody and Billy Graham is the simplicity of their message. Consistently, these men have focused on Jesus Christ through the use of just a few very fundamental truths. And their simple message brought millions into God's kingdom.

Yet sometimes we Christians are often guilty of making the gospel presentation so boring and cumbersome that we fail to communicate the essentials of God's Word. There are so many Scriptures to choose from, and so many comments we can add to these Scriptures, that it is difficult to know what to include and what to leave for later.

As Vonette and I launched the ministry of Campus Crusade at UCLA in 1951, we learned that college students—whether they majored in physical education or philosophy—were not impressed with complex communications of the gospel. What impressed them was Jesus Christ—who He is, what He did for them, and how they can know Him personally. So we concentrated on the death and resurrection of our Lord (see 1 Cor 2:2).

During the first years of the ministry, we gave a studied effort to making the gospel presentation as clear and simple as we possibly could. God blessed the effort, and we saw student leaders, All-America athletes, fraternity and sorority officers, professors, and college officials come to Christ.

76 – Is Faith Private?

"I don't wear my religion on my sleeve. My religion is personal and private, and I don't talk about it."

He was one of America's great statesmen, and I had just shared with him a plan for world evangelism. As we talked about involving a thousand key Christian leaders in the effort, his statement startled me.

"You're a Christian, aren't you?" I asked.

"Yes," he replied. "But I'm not a religious fanatic."

I have heard this logic several times, but it still grieves me every time I hear it. So I prodded him gently, "Did it ever occur to you that it cost Jesus Christ His life so that you could say you're a Christian?"

He thought for a moment, but did not respond.

"It cost the disciples their lives," I continued. "Millions of Christians throughout the centuries have suffered and died to get the message of God's love and forgiveness to you. Now do you really believe that your faith in Christ is private and that you shouldn't talk about it?"

"No, sir," the man sighed. "I'm wrong. Tell me what I can do about it."

Without realizing it, this Christian leader had fallen for one of Satan's favorite lines: your faith is a private matter. Therefore, his witness for Christ was almost nil. He held in his possession the greatest news ever announced, but he had refused to share it.

Paul commands us to take the news of Jesus Christ everywhere (see Col 1:28). Let us not keep the joyful news to ourselves!

77 – The Golden Years

Our culture offers two views on aging. One says that retirees should gradually pull away from former pursuits. I am sure you have heard older Christians remark, "I've served the Lord for many years. Now it's time for me to sit back and let younger people take over."

The other view says that senior citizens must remain active at all costs. The elderly are not much different than middle-aged adults. Except for slowing down somewhat, older persons should work and participate in other activities as they once did. Both views have some truth to them, within balance.

God regards the elderly with high honor (see Lv 19:32). In recent years, Vonette and I have felt burdened for that strategic segment of society who possess the phenomenal, even revolutionary potential for serving God—those sixty years and older. We envision many older couples and singles serving Christ in ways they never dreamed possible. We see them growing and learning through their retirement years, and using their talents and skills until the end of their lives.

God may change our ministry as we grow older, but He never asks us to retire from His work. At every age, we must be open to His calling. If you are approaching the golden years, I encourage you to ask God how you can serve Him as you grow older. If you are younger, I urge you to take advantage of the decades of experience and maturity that senior adults offer your ministry.

78 – The Most Important Information

What would you consider the most important information you could ever study and apply in your life? What is so foundational that it undergirds everything in your relationship to God and even to other people? What more than anything else should motivate you to love, trust, and obey God?

Many years ago, I was interviewed by Dr. James Boice of the Bible Hour. One of the first questions he asked me was, "What is the most important truth to teach believers?" No one had ever asked me that question, and I was totally unprepared for it. I am convinced the Holy Spirit gave me the answer, "The attributes of God."

I have had years to think about that question, and I am more convinced now than ever that there is nothing more important to teach believers than what God is really like. Our view of God determines our lifestyle. What we believe to be true about God's character affects our friendships, work and leisure, the friends we choose, the type of literature we read, and even the music to which we listen.

Everything about our lives, attitudes, motives, desires, actions, and even our words are determined and influenced by our view of God. There are no convictions in life that are more important to victorious living than what we believe to be true about God. I challenge you to search the Scriptures to know "the Sovereign Lord ... in all his glorious power" (Is 40:10, NLT).

79 – The Character of God

Through the years, I have meditated on the character of our awesome God. I ask Him to saturate my thought life with His wisdom and release His power in me through the Holy Spirit.

Several months ago, while I was writing about the attributes of God, I was overcome with a sense of my unworthiness to write about the great character qualities of God. Who am I—Bill Bright, sinful and depraved from conception? And I am trying to write about the great God of the universe who is all-powerful, holy, and righteous! I remember falling to my knees in tears and confessing to God, "Oh Lord, I am not worthy to write about Your character. Forgive me for even being so presumptuous."

I readily admit that as a human being, I am incapable of completely explaining God. However, we base our knowledge of God on the inerrant, proven Word of God. We also understand God by how He interacts with people and nations throughout history.

In Psalms God says, "Be silent, and know that I am God! I will be honored by every nation. I will be honored throughout the world." (Ps 46:10, NLT). One of the greatest things we can do in our lifetime is get to know Him better, the holiness of His nature, His power and justice, and His love. Once we know Him, we will have a better focus on our part in His plan for eternity and His glorious love for us as our heavenly Father.

80 – Four of God's Qualities

Our God is gloriously incomprehensible. Psalm 46 says, "God is the King over all the earth. Praise Him with a psalm!" (see Ps 46:7). Let us briefly consider four qualities of God which are completely foreign to our understanding.

First, He is infinite. That means God has no limits, no boundaries, no ending. He cannot be measured or compared to any finite standard. Everything within our world is finite. Only God is infinite.

God is self-existent. He had no beginning. He was not created. Everything in the universe had a beginning, except God. Because He is the Creator, He is the only One who exists outside of the created order.

God is eternal. He is not bound by the dimensions of time and space. He has no end. Before He spoke the first word of creation, time did not exist. He created time as a temporary context for His creation. All of history is but a little speck within the spectrum of eternity. And God encompasses all of eternity!

God is self-sufficient. He has no needs. He is dependent upon nothing outside Himself. All of creation relies upon God for existence and the maintenance of life. But God has no need for anything. He is not vulnerable in any way. He does not need our help. He only offers us the privilege of being involved with Him in the fulfillment of His purposes.

Yes, our glorious God is truly incomprehensible. We will never be able to fully understand His magnificence.

81 – Mercy in Our Sinfulness

If there is one thing I have learned over the years, God shows mercy to us in our sinfulness. Daniel exclaimed, "The Lord our God is merciful and forgiving, even though we have rebelled against him" (Dn 9:9, NIV).

Some years ago, I was invited to speak to the inmates of one of the most infamous high-security prisons in America, the Federal Penitentiary in Atlanta, Georgia. When I arrived at the Penitentiary Assembly Room, several of the inmates rushed over to me, embraced me, and called me "brother." They told me they had heard my messages on tape, read my books, and had been helped by them.

Before I spoke, several stood and testified how they had been forgiven by God through faith in Christ's death and resurrection. One man told how he had murdered five people. Another confessed to killing three. Others had committed similar crimes. They had come to the prison full of hate and fear—then they met Jesus and were transformed.

Tears streamed down my face as I listened to these testimonies of God's mercy and love. Again and again different ones said, "I'm glad I'm here. If I had not been sent to prison, I would not know Christ, and I would probably be dead because of my life of crime."

These prisoners had experienced the wonder of God's eternal pardon from their sins. They had received peace of heart and mind. They were experiencing purpose and meaning for their lives—even in their prison cells.

82 – God Never Fails

God will never fail us! The more we understand this, the less room we have in our hearts for worry.

In Pakistan, during a time of great political upheaval, Vonette and I had finished a series of meetings and were taken to the train station. I was unaware that an angry crowd of thousands was marching on the station to destroy it with cocktail bombs. The director of the railway line rushed us to our compartments and told us not to open our doors under any circumstances.

As I put on my pajamas for the night, a peace filled my heart. I knew the Lord was with Vonette and me and our party and would protect us from all harm. It was not until we arrived in Karachi some twenty-eight hours later that I discovered how guardian angels had watched over us. The train before us had been burned when rioting students had lain on the track and refused to move. The train ran over them and, in retaliation, the mob burned the train and killed the officials.

Our train was next to arrive. The angry mob was prepared to do the same to us. But God miraculously went before us, and we arrived safely in Karachi to discover that martial law had been declared and all was peaceful.

Truly, God faithfully responds to prayers such as David's: "O Lord, hear my prayer, listen to my cry for mercy; in your faithfulness and righteousness come to my relief" (Ps 143:1, NIV).

83 – We Can Trust God

Recently, I boarded a plane in Europe bound for the United States. A man I had never seen before—whose name I didn't even know—boarded the same plane, entered the captain's cabin and seated himself at the controls. A short time later, the aircraft began to move, and by some means that I do not understand, it left the ground. Hours later we touched down in Orlando.

Not once during our flight did it occur to me to question the man at the controls. I never thought to ask to see his pilot's license or some identification to prove he was capable of flying that plane. I never asked him to explain to me the physical laws by which he could keep such a heavy object in the air. Yet, from the very moment I boarded that plane, I placed my faith in that stranger, believing he was capable of taking me safely to my destination.

Every day, in hundreds of similar situations, believers and nonbelievers alike exercise faith without even thinking twice. If we have such unquestioning faith in fellow human beings—who are not only fallible, but also deliberately sinful and even unfaithful at times—how much more should we put all of our faith in God, whose character and capabilities for faithfulness are beyond question?

The writer of Hebrews declares, "God can be trusted to keep His promises" (Heb 10:23, NLT). God is trustworthy. He cannot be otherwise. Our holy and loving God is faithful!

84 – God Created Everything Out of Nothing

If you've traveled by air and gone into the gift shops at airports, you will have seen some lovely pottery on display. If you go through Phoenix, almost all the pottery on display has a southwestern motif. Yet as you admire that, your mind does not stop with the beautiful shape of the pottery, you think of the person who made it.

Yet have you ever wondered who made the clay that the potter used to shape his creation? Certainly not the potter, who probably ordered in a shipment of clean, usable clay before he started on his project.

That is, however, not what happened when God made the earth and the heavens and everything in it. As the Master Creator, He made everything out of nothing—nothing! We read, "By the word of the Lord were the heavens made, their starry host by the breath of his mouth" (Ps 33:6, NIV). The apostle John, speaking of Jesus Christ, wrote, "Through him all things were made; without him nothing was made that has been made" (Jn 1:3, NIV). And the apostle Paul exclaims: "For by him all things were created: things in heaven and on earth, visible and invisible, whether thrones or powers or rulers or authorities; all things were created by him and for him" (Col 1:16, NIV). That is right. There was nothing when He started, but when God spoke, the sky was filled with stars. That is power! All power!

85 – A Balance of Justice and Compassion

We can trust God to act in every situation—in His timing. The account of David being chased by King Saul is an example. David, who had already been anointed as the future king, was running for his life from King Saul. Then the moment came when David had his chance to right a wrong.

David and his people had settled deep into a cave for the night when King Saul and his men encamped in the front of the cave. David crept up to where King Saul lay and cut off a corner of the king's robe. He could have killed King Saul, but he did not (see 1 Sm 24:4).

David's men were angry, for they were convinced God had placed King Saul into their hands to set things right. After all, none of the king's men would have known who had run a spear through the body of the sleeping king and killed him. But David explained to his men that he simply could not do it, that it was not right because the king was still God's anointed.

What was behind David's reasoning? The Psalms give us the answer. He believed that a righteous God would take care of King Saul—and in God's sovereign, divine time He would set up David as the king. David's view of the righteousness of God prompted him to wait upon God to act. David's God clearly reflected a righteous God's balance of love and compassion, of justice and wrath against sin.

86 – Getting to Know God

On our own, we cannot understand or know God. The relationship must be initiated on His side. Because God is so far above us in every way, the process begins with Him as He reveals Himself to us. The Bible gives us the most accurate picture of the almighty God and His role as a heavenly Father.

The first way God reveals Himself in the Bible is as the powerful Creator. Genesis 1, the first chapter in the Bible, lays out the Creator's almighty works and His unlimited power.

Then God reveals His depth of integrity. The remainder of the Old Testament shows how God built a nation of people dedicated to Him and how He led these people and the laws and promises that establish God's nature as one of holiness and integrity.

Last, in the New Testament God reveals Himself as a loving heavenly Father by sending His Son to earth as Savior of the world. Jesus is the flesh-and-blood proof of God's love, mercy, and faithfulness.

The most astounding news we can ever hear is that God, the almighty Creator of heaven and earth, invites us to have an intimate relationship with Him. He makes it simple for us to do so. By taking a few practical steps to knowing God intimately such as studying His Word, asking to be filled with His Spirit, and walking daily in His light, our lives will be transformed into ones of passion, joy, adventure, and peace.

87 – Miraculous Answer to Prayer

Our ministry has grown worldwide simply because God has not changed in how He has cared for us. When we were still quite small I was informed one day that we had an urgent need for $485. Since we did not have any surplus funds, I began to pray about this need.

I was alone in my office that Saturday morning, praying, when I heard a knock on the door. I debated briefly if I should interrupt my time of prayer to answer it. I reached the door just as the mailman was leaving. He said, "It's a good thing you are here, or I would not have been able to leave this letter."

I signed for the letter and went back to my office to continue praying. Then I felt impressed to open the letter. Inside, I discovered a bank note for $500 sent by a friend from Zurich, Switzerland. His entire family had become Christians through our ministry and now he was expressing his gratitude.

I had prayed in faith, expecting God to answer. He did—before I actually voiced my prayer. He had moved upon the heart of this friend in Zurich many days before.

Through the years I have seen God, in response to our faith, provide finances on thousands of occasions. In addition, He gave us peace of mind and heart as He met our need. That unchanging response of God to our prayers built an incredible faith in His faithfulness, willingness, and ability to meet our need.

88 – God's Perspective

When you fly from Chicago to Los Angeles on some airlines you will fly over one section of the Grand Canyon. If you happen to fly over it during the late afternoon sun, the canyon's shadows help you see the incredible depth and breadth of it. But the fact remains—you are seeing only a small segment of it, for it runs well over a thousand miles.

Now imagine yourself circling the earth in the Mir space station and you come over the Grand Canyon. How much of it will you see now? All of it in one glance, would you not?

When we look at life on earth we see a minute sliver of it, one miniscule slice of eternity. I describe it as looking at a parade through a keyhole. But God can see the end from the beginning because He is from everlasting to everlasting. That is why we need God's perspective on the events of life—He sees it in ways we do not and as a result He can take corrective action when we turn our life unreservedly over to Him.

What a great God we have! We can trust Him not to turn against us, for His love is unchanging. We can trust Him for life after death, for He is eternal. That's why the writer of Hebrews could say: "Jesus Christ is the same yesterday and today and forever" (Heb 13:8, NIV). He watches over us from His vantage point in heaven. What greater perspective could we ever ask for our lives?

Soviet Union, 1978

89 – God's Infinity

One day, St. Augustine, a leader in the early Church, was walking along the ocean shore pondering God's nature when he noticed a small boy playing in the sand. The child scooped a hole in the sand with a seashell. Then he ran down to the water's edge and dipped his shell full of seawater. Immediately, he ran back and dumped the water into the hole he had made in the sand. Of course, the water just leaked out.

Augustine asked the boy, "What are you doing?"

With confidence, the boy replied, "I am going to pour the sea into that hole."

"Ah," Augustine reflected, "that is what I have been trying to do. Standing at the ocean of infinity, I have attempted to grasp it with my finite mind."

Who can understand God's infinity? Isaiah writes, "Who has measured the waters in the hollow of His hand, and marked off the heavens by the span, and calculated the dust of the earth by the measure, and weighed the mountains in a balance, and the hills in a pair of scales?" (Is 40:12, NASB)[40].

God's infinity means that He has no limits, no boundaries, no ending. Everything within our world is finite—even the universe. God and only God is infinite. And this quality relates to all of God's attributes which means that His love, holiness, mercy, and all His qualities are unlimited in their scope and expression.

90 – Our In-Control God

How would you like to live in a world where everyone could do whatever he wanted? Can you imagine the chaos? I have been in countries which seem to have no traffic laws. Taxi drivers go at break-neck speed, often colliding with each other. Fortunately, I have not been in a taxi when a collision has occurred. I certainly would not want to drive to work each day if I did not know which direction the other cars were going!

Sometimes this world seems just as chaotic and out-of-control, yet God is in control of the future. When we look at the universe, we see order and design. Everything is in its place; everything has its purpose. If creation has so much purpose and design, then human history must also have purpose and design.

But many people are skeptical about God's willingness to get intimately involved in the affairs of men. They may agree that God has a general purpose for everything, but question whether particular events are really part of His will.

In His Word, however, God shows that He has a plan for this world and every person in it. God's Word says that God has plans for nations and rulers. Psalm 66:5,7 records, "Come and see what God has done, how awesome his works in man's behalf!... He rules forever by his power, his eyes watch the nation" (NIV).

No matter what happens anywhere in the world at any moment, God is always in control. This is a comforting truth.

91 – God Is Always With Us

When I awaken in the morning, God is with me. When I kneel to worship Him, He is with me. When I arrive at the office, or at the airport for one of my many trips, He is still with me.

God is with me when I am on the airplane, and He is with me when I arrive at my destination, whether in California, Pakistan, or Brazil. He is with me as I turn out the lights at night anywhere in the world. He is with every one of our 225,000 full-time and trained staff members in more than 200 countries of the world.

Jesus promises, "Surely I am with you always, to the very end of the age" (Mt 28:20, NIV). This is part of the Great Commission—the challenge to go into all the world and preach the gospel, discipling those who come to faith in Christ. It is when we are fulfilling the Great Commission that Jesus' promise to be with us becomes most precious. We can be confident that Christ is present with believers in the United States, Canada, Germany, Russia, Indonesia, Egypt, Venezuela—and every other country and culture at the same time.

God is not limited by time or space or height or depth. He is always with us whether we can take giant steps or the first baby steps of faith. He lives inside of every person who puts his trust in God through faith in Jesus Christ.

92 – A Consistent Prayer Life

I encourage you to make the time you spend with Jesus the richest part of your day. If we are in love with Jesus, we will want to talk to Him many times each day. Moment by moment fellowship with Jesus Christ enables us to gain insight into God's will for our lives (see Ps 3:1-3).

Like a vibrant spreading tree, our spirit grows strong and healthy when we consistently read, study, memorize, and meditate on God's holy Word. A consistent prayer life also keeps us in touch with the Source of our success. No one knew this better than Jesus who spent much time alone with His heavenly Father. Matthew 14:23 says, "Then afterwards he went up into the hills to pray" (TLB). If you read through the Gospels, you will find many other times when He went away alone to pray. One of the most well-known examples is His prayer in the Garden of Gethsemane just before He was taken away to be crucified. He was preparing Himself for the ordeal He knew He had to go through during the next few days.

His example illustrates the importance of prayer and meditation in building a vital relationship with God. Talking to Jesus about everything you do and asking Him to reveal anything in your life that is displeasing to Him will give you a clear channel of communication with the Source of your fulfillment.

93 – The Two Most Important Questions

All over the world, I have asked two questions of millions of Christians—young and old, rich and poor, new Christians and people who have been believers for more than half a century. I have asked these questions of some of the most wealthy and famous Christians in the world. Their answers are always the same:

Question: What is the most important experience of your life?

Answer: "Knowing Christ as my Savior is absolutely the most important experience in my life."

Question: What is the most important thing that you can do to help another person?

Answer: "Help him to know Christ."

I am sure you would give the same answers to these questions. Jesus calls to every believer, "Follow me, and I will make you fishers of men" (Mt 4:19). Shortly before He left the earth, He gave what is commonly referred to as the Great Commission (see Mt 28:16-20). The Great Commission is simply bringing God's message to others, introducing them to our Lord and Savior, Jesus Christ, then helping them grow in His love. Helping to fulfill the Great Commission is the greatest purpose you and I can have as Christians.

Billions of people around the world have yet to hear the name of Jesus. I urge you to share the message of God's love and forgiveness through Jesus Christ with everyone who will listen.

94 – Invest in God's Work

Much of what we accumulate—our wealth, power, and prestige—will be transferred to others when we die. Most of us including our accomplishments, wealth, etc. will be forgotten soon after we die. What people will remember is the model of our life and witness for our Lord. Those whom we help introduce to Christ and disciple for His glory through our personal witness and financial investments will carry our legacy generation after generation long after our lifetime.

As Christians, all that we have, we possess by the grace and gift of God. Psalm 24:1 says, "The earth is the Lord's, and everything in it, the world, and all who live in it" (NIV). God is pleased when we give generously to His work out of the resources He has entrusted to us.

Every Christian should consider how he can use his finances to help win and disciple the largest number of people for Christ. Since everything we have belongs to God, we give, not as a requirement, but as an act of loving obedience and worship to our Savior and Lord.

Do you have a systematic plan for giving? Let me suggest a minimum of 10 percent of your income—called a tithe—as a realistic starting point. Then be open to His leading in giving above this amount for special needs and opportunities that come your way. I challenge you to give generously for six months to see how God will multiply the fruit of your gifts in the lives of others.

95 – Praying in Jesus' Name

God honors those who truly pray in His Son's name. We have double assurance of this.

First, our Lord said that the heavenly Father will grant our requests when we ask in Jesus' name. "You won't need to ask me for anything, for you can go directly to the Father and ask him, and he will give you what you ask for because you use my name" (Jn 16:23, TLB).

Second, Jesus Himself will give us what we ask in His name so He can glorify the Father. "Anyone who has faith in me will do what I have been doing. He will do even greater things than these, because I am going to the Father. And I will do whatever you ask in my name, so that the Son may bring glory to the Father. You may ask me for anything in my name, and I will do it" (Jn 14:12-14, NIV).

But "in Jesus' name" is not a magical phrase to be tacked onto the end of our prayers for special effect. Too often we speak those words in meaningless, glib benediction. And we wonder why our prayers have no power, why our petitions go unanswered.

We must use the name of Jesus with understanding and integrity. All that Jesus is, is wrapped up in His name. His nature, His attributes, His Word, His glory, His mission on earth—all must harmonize when we truly pray "in Jesus' name."

96 – Keeping First Love Fresh

Imagine the Christian life as a marathon. The starting gun sounds when the racer accepts Christ as his Savior and Lord. With a burst of speed, the runner heads down the track with enthusiasm, heart pumping.

A couple of hours into the race, he is barely recognizable. His face sags, his feet drag, and he pants with every step. As he passes a shady park bench, he stops to rest a moment. Soon he is dozing in the cool breeze. He has lost sight of the prize awaiting those who finish the race.

Many Christians live their lives like this racer. They begin their Christian life with zeal. They genuinely love Christ and produce much fruit for Him. But as they allow the burden of running the race to overwhelm their daily lives, they begin to stray from the path of devotion. They are like the Christians in the early church of Ephesus who were known for their good works and patience but who had abandoned their first love for the Lord. To that church, Jesus said, "You don't love me as at first! Think about those times of your first love (how different now!) and turn back to me again and work as you did before" (Rv 2:4,5, TLB).

If you find you have left your first love, confess your lukewarmness as sin and appropriate God's forgiveness and cleansing. Then claim by faith the restoration of your love for God and the fullness of the Holy Spirit.

97 – You Can Be Sure You Are a Christian

If you have received Christ as Savior, sometimes you may wonder if you really are a Christian. You may say, "I believe Jesus Christ is the Son of God and died for my sins. Yet I don't feel like a child of God."

How, then, can you be sure that you are a Christian? Is there some kind of confirmation that God gives to those who sincerely receive Christ? I believe there is a threefold confirmation that Jesus Christ is in your life.

1. External witness of God's Word

The promise of God's Word, not your feelings, is your authority (see 1 Jn 5:11,12). His Word is totally reliable. As a Christian, you are to live by faith in the trustworthiness of God and His holy, inspired Word. Memorize it and repeat it whenever you doubt your relationship to Christ.

2. Internal witness of the Holy Spirit

Paul writes, "The Spirit himself testifies with our spirit that we are God's children" (Rom 8:16, NIV). Paul emphasized the validity of this inner source of assurance in 1 Thessalonians 1:5.

3. Changed life

Your changed life is a witness to the fact that you are a Christian. Paul records, "When someone becomes a Christian he becomes a brand new person inside. He is not the same person anymore. A new life has begun!" (2 Cor 5:17, TLB).

Jesus would not deceive you. You can be sure, if you asked Him into your life, He now lives inside you and will give you the abundant life He promised.

98 – Loving by Faith

For years, I had spoken on the subject of love. But, as in the case of most sermons on love, something was missing. I still did not grasp one essential ingredient for enabling God to love through me—despite the circumstances.

One night, I was awakened at 2 A.M. I knew that God had something to say to me. I felt impressed to get out of bed, take my Bible, and go into another room so I would not disturb Vonette. I fell to my knees and read and prayed for the next couple of hours.

What I discovered that night has since enriched my life. It was so simple, so biblical, and so revolutionary. The discovery? *Christians can love by faith.*

Truly, love is the greatest privilege and power known to man. When Christ came into my life and I became a Christian, God gave me the resources to be a different person. He gave me the ability to love.

Everything in the Christian life, I knew, was based on faith. Hebrews 11:6 says, "*Without faith* it is impossible to please Him" (NASB, italics mine). We love by faith just as we received Christ by faith, just as we are filled with the Holy Spirit by faith, and just as we walk in the Spirit by faith. Love is an act of our will and not emotions. Because we are obeying God's command to love (see Jn 15:12), we are not being hypocritical when we say, "I love you" even though we may not feel like loving. Love is first a decision—a commitment—followed by loving acts and then comes the feelings.

99 – The Most Remarkable Person

Jesus is the most remarkable and fascinating person in history. He has inspired more hope, taught more compassion, and shown more love than any other man who has ever lived.

When He walked on earth, Jesus stirred people wherever He went. Crowds followed Him; hands reached out to Him; voices called to Him; people pushed and sometimes trampled one another just to see Him, to hear Him teach, to bring their sick to be healed.

Jesus' popularity grew until many wanted to make Him king of the Jews. Once, when He entered Jerusalem, the capital city of Israel, crowds lining the wayside pulled off their cloaks and broke off palm branches to throw in front of Him. When He entered Jerusalem, the whole city took notice. People gathered asking, "Who is this man?"

Others answered, "This is the prophet, Jesus, from Nazareth" (Mt 21:9-11).

Indeed, there has never been anyone who could compare with Jesus of Nazareth. He is unique among all the human beings who have ever been born. Wherever the true message of Jesus Christ has gone, people and nations have been revolutionized, resulting in new life, new hope, and new purpose for living. Indeed, without the fear of contradiction, we can regard Jesus Christ as history's greatest revolutionary. Everything about Him was unique: the prophecies of His coming. His birth. His life. His teachings. His miracles. His death. His resurrection. His influence on history and in the lives of hundreds of millions of people.

100 – Proofs of the Resurrection

The validity of Jesus' claims about Himself rests on the resurrection—whether He rose from the dead or stayed in the grave. On my spiritual journey from agnosticism to a vital, living faith in Christ, I had a problem with the resurrection. How could a human being who had died be raised from the dead? I was willing to believe, but not at the risk of losing my intellectual integrity. So I investigated the evidences.

My personal study brought me to a firm conviction that a bodily resurrection is the only explanation for Christ's empty tomb. Five evidences helped me reach this conclusion.

1. Christ predicted His resurrection (see Mt 16:21).
2. He made numerous appearances to His followers after His resurrection. (see Mt 28:1-10; Lk 24:13-32; 1 Cor 15:3-6).
3. The unrelenting faith of the disciples. Those who were once so afraid that they deserted our Lord now risked their lives to preach the facts of the resurrection of Jesus.
4. The growth of the Christian church. The small group of first century believers multiplied until it now reaches around the world.
5. The testimony of hundreds of millions of transformed lives through the centuries.

The resurrection sets Christianity apart from all religions. No religion can claim that its founder was raised from the dead and lives today in the hearts of His followers. No other religious leader has broken the power of death and conquered sin. Only Christianity is based on the historical evidence of a risen Savior and an empty tomb.

101 – The Power of the Holy Spirit

I know without a doubt that, had I not learned early in my Christian experience of my personal need for the Holy Spirit, I would have made a mess of my life. By nature I am rather shy and reserved. Talking with people about Jesus Christ does not always come easily for me. Yet, in over five decades of ministry, the Holy Spirit has given me boldness to share Christ effectively, as well as an ability to train other Christians to do likewise.

In the course of leading a worldwide ministry, I have experienced the Holy Spirit's direction when it appeared that all options were closed. He has given me patience and peace when deadlines or financial obligations appeared impossible to meet. He has filled me with joy when my natural reaction would have been anger or despair.

I cannot accept accolades for any success in my personal ministry or for the success of Campus Crusade for Christ, for I know that if I do not allow Him to direct me day by day, all my efforts for Christ will be futile. But when I earnestly seek to yield to His guidance, I am confident that the very gates of hell cannot prevail against the ministry He wants to have in and through me.

The power of the Holy Spirit is available to you—right now! Your walk with God will take on a new dimension of purpose and power when you let the Holy Spirit do His work in your life!

Overtly or covertly, Satan's goal is to rob you of the joy of your relationship with Jesus Christ. He wants you to dishonor God by being spiritually inconsistent, unhappy, lethargic. He wants to keep you from attracting and introducing others to our Lord.

As he goes about his task, he will come at you in some appealing ways:

- An extramarital opportunity for emotional or sexual release.
- A growing resentment, perhaps in the name of righteousness, toward a fellow worker or church member.
- An opportunity to display your wit through negativism or cynicism.
- Getting so busy doing the *work* of the Lord that you ignore your *walk* with the Lord.

Over the years, Satan has come at me with many of these temptations. I am sure that in years to come he will dangle many more before me. It is humbling and sobering to know that, even after almost fifty years as a Christian, I am susceptible to any one of the enemy's tactics if I do not rely totally on God's loving power moment by moment.

But I can testify wholeheartedly that, while God in His sovereign way allows the conflict between good and evil to go on, He provides each of us with the ultimate weapon against Satan—the life-giving Spirit (see Rom 7:25–8:4).

Through the power of the Spirit, we will do great things in His name, resist the pull of the kingdom of darkness, live a life that brings honor to Him, and the joy and fulfillment to us.

103 – The Divine Mystery

Our best efforts to explain the Trinity fall far short. I might say that as a man I am also a husband, a father, and the president of a worldwide ministry. One man, three functions. Or I could say that H_2O is three different things: liquid, ice, or steam. One formula, three forms. But the Trinity is far greater than these awkward illustrations.

What we do know from God's Word is that we have one God who manifests Himself in three distinct persons. Charles Ryrie notes that when Jesus said, "I and the Father are one" (Jn 10:30, NIV), He used the neuter form of *one*, which "rules out the meaning that [the Father and Son] are one person." Rather, the meaning is that "the Father and Son [and it follows, the Holy Spirit] are in perfect unity in their natures and actions."*

All three have the mind and attributes of God, so there is never conflict or disagreement among the three. The three are one; the one is three. Later in the same conversation, Jesus said, "The Father is in me, and I in the Father" (Jn 10:38, NIV). Indeed, a divine mystery.

One of my seminary professors once said, "To try to understand the Trinity is to lose one's mind; to deny the Trinity is to lose one's soul." The Trinity will never be comprehended on human terms, but that should not preclude our wholehearted reliance on its existence.

---

*Charles C. Ryrie, *The Ryrie Study Bible (NAS)* (Chicago: Moody Press, 1978), footnote to John 10:30.

104 – Shifting the Focus

Just a few days ago, an assistant brought me news of a problem that had arisen in our preparations for a major worldwide evangelistic campaign we were spearheading in cooperation with thousands of churches and Christian organizations. Any undertaking this large encounters snags, and this particular problem was neither the first nor the last.

But upon hearing the news, my first reaction was to praise God that He is bigger than any problems I might ever encounter. ("Is anything too difficult for the Lord?" God asked Abraham rhetorically in Genesis 18:14, NASB.) Through five decades of ministry, He has answered our prayers and met our needs so many times that I have learned to place my total confidence in Him—even when a solution seems humanly impossible.

In this situation, the act of praising His glorious name moved our focus off the problem and onto the problem-solver, our powerful Savior. We then asked Him for wisdom, and that His Holy Spirit would guide us as we discussed possible solutions.

I do not respond this way every time—my sinful nature can still cause trouble. But as I have grown in the Lord and allowed Him to guide me through His Spirit, His supernatural joy and peace have become more and more a part of me. The Spirit of God pours out an ample supply of optimism from within so that generally my first reaction to adversity is one of genuine joy and peace.

105 – The Power of Gentleness

Gentleness is humility born of strength and confidence. It is the quiet, moving power of the understatement. It is what enabled our Lord to act as though He were thinking, *I am strong enough to be overbearing, and I am strong enough to be gentle. I choose to be gentle.*

His gentleness changed the world.

There is tremendous power in gentleness. As a young businessman, I had the opportunity to talk briefly with J.C. Penney, the department store mogul who commanded thousands of employees and millions of dollars across the country. As we visited, I was impressed that Penney was one of the most gentle and humble men I had ever met.

A devoted Christian, he built the J.C. Penney department store chain on the Golden Rule: "Do unto others as you would have them do unto you." He showed this young businessman the incredible power of gentleness in human relationships.

As I have grown older, I realized that arrogance and boastfulness are the traits of insecure, self-important men and women. Arrogance has no place in the Christian life, for our Lord said, "Blessed are the gentle, for they shall inherit the earth" (Mt 5:5, NAS).

He was talking about the gentleness that becomes a part of us when we are filled with the Holy Spirit—the gentleness of a strong, quietly confident person who acknowledges that Jesus Christ is the source of his strength.

If you lack gentleness, confess your sin, appropriate God's forgiveness, and trust God to fill you with gentleness.

106 – Fact, Faith, and Feelings

When you received Christ, you may or may not have had an emotional experience. Feelings are not what save us; God's Word says we are saved through faith (see Eph 2:8).

God also instructs us to live each day in the same way: "As you therefore have received Christ Jesus the Lord, so walk in Him" (Col 2:6, NAS). On some occasions, such as a particular joyful or convicting or heartbreaking situation, we may become emotional. But for the most part, we may not feel deeply ecstatic or emotional.

We can compare facts, faith, and feeling to a train. The engine (FACT) signifies that the promise of God's Word—not our feelings—is our authority and guide for the Christian life. The coal car (FAITH) signifies the fuel that brings action to the facts. We are to live by faith in the trustworthiness of God Himself and His Word. The caboose represents our FEELINGS. Our emotions should be the *result* of our faith, not a *cause* of our faith.

The train will run with or without the caboose. However, it would be useless to try to pull the train by the caboose. In the same way, we as Christians are not to depend on feelings or emotions—we must place our trust in the trustworthiness of God and His promises. Feelings will vary, but the *fact* of God's trustworthiness remains constant.

107 – Prayer Is a Discipline

We have the amazing privilege of talking directly with the omnipotent God. He is more accessible to us than our doctor or dentist! We do not need to set up an appointment for three weeks from Friday, nor is there any time limit on our conversations with Him. He is always there, always ready to listen. Prayer is one of the ways God has provided for us to seek His mind and know His will.

Dwight L. Moody said, "The Christian on his knees sees more than the philosopher on tiptoe." Thus, prayer is a key discipline for the Christian who wants to live with purpose and power.

God desires a closer, more intimate communion with His children that goes far deeper than merely giving Him a wish list. Unhurried prayer—in which we praise and thank God, intercede for others, ask for His wisdom and listen for His guidance—demonstrates our love for Him and our desire to seek His mind in all things. Jesus exercised the daily discipline of communication with His heavenly Father; He was the Son of God, yet He made prayer top priority!

Prayer is a discipline—but it is also a matchless privilege! According to Philippians 4:6, God wants us to talk to Him about *everything*.

Please do not treat lightly the discipline and privilege of prayer. Just as unrushed, in-depth conversation with a spouse or friend draws you closer to that person, so will unhurried and honest conversation with God draw you nearer to Him.

108 – God Holds Our Hand

Vonette and I were wading down a shallow stream in Yosemite Park with our two young sons. Because the rocks were slippery, I was holding my five-year-old, Bradley, by the hand to keep him from slipping on the rocks.

Suddenly Brad did slip, and his feet went out from under him. Fortunately I was holding his hand. I held him firmly until he regained his balance. Had he fallen he could have been seriously injured.

As we continued our walk, Brad looked up into my face with a radiant expression of gratitude. "Daddy," he said, "I'm sure glad you kept me from falling."

In the flash of a moment, it was as though God had spoken to me through Brad. I looked upward and said to my Father in heaven, "Father, I'm so glad You have kept me from falling; on thousands of occasions You have kept me from falling."

We walked in silence for a few moments. Then Brad looked up into my face again with that kind of expression that melts the heart of a father. "Daddy," he said, "I'm glad you're holding my hand." This time tears came to my eyes as I said to my Father in heaven, "I'm so glad You hold me by the hand; I'm so prone to fall."

Oh, this supernatural life is wonderful! Exciting! As Jesus says in John 10:10, it is filled with adventure for those who let God control their lives—who walk with Him, moment by moment, day by day, allowing Him to "hold their hands."

109 – Simple and Understandable

Some years ago, while speaking at the University of Houston, I was told about a brilliant philosophy major. He was so gifted that even the professors were impressed by his ability to comprehend quickly and to debate nationally. He was an atheist and had a way of embarrassing the Christians who tried to witness to him.

I was asked to talk with him about Christ. We sat in a booth in the student center, talking about his philosophy of life and the Word of God. He successfully monopolized the conversation with his philosophy of unbelief in God.

At every opportunity, I reminded him that God loved him and offered him a wonderful plan for his life. I showed him various Scripture passages, underlining the importance of his turning to God. He seemed to ignore everything I said.

After a couple of hours, I felt there was no need to continue the discussion, so we agreed to call it a day. As we got in the car, his first words were, "Everything you said tonight hit me right in the heart. I want to receive Christ. Tell me how I can do it right now." Even though I had not sensed it during our conversation, the Holy Spirit had been speaking to his heart through God's Word.

Learn to use the Word of God. Do not try to impress people with your brilliance, logic, or persuasiveness. There are no valid arguments against the Word of God when it is presented in the power of the Holy Spirit (see 1 Tm 1:8).

110 – Satan Is a Defeated Foe

A story appeared in the press about a soldier who had been wounded and separated from the rest of his company in the jungles of a South Sea island. The soldier had to hunt for food, water, and shelter, and he was in constant fear of being captured or killed by enemy patrols.

For two years, the soldier avoided his enemy. Finally he stumbled upon some soldiers from his own country near the edge of a village. With joy, he quickly told them his story and asked if the enemy had finally been driven off the island. The men told him that the war had been over for a long time and that his country had won.

This story is similar to what often happens in the life of a Christian. Like the soldier, many Christians are living in defeat and fear because they do not know that victory has been won in the conflict with Satan. Such Christians live in fear of Satan.

They try to fight the battle alone, and become separated from God. They feel defeated, frustrated, and confused. Their attitude would change if only they knew that they are already on the winning side.

Satan was defeated 2,000 years ago when Christ died on the cross for our sins (see 1 Jn 4:4). Though Satan has great power to influence, he only has that power which has been granted to him by God. He is a defeated foe.

111 – The Supernatural Power of Faith

Occasionally, I hear people say that "Bill Bright is a man of great faith." The statement is made because our ministry frequently is involved with many thousands of churches of all denominations and other Christian organizations in gargantuan undertakings—massive worldwide programs of evangelism and discipleship in which we have by faith trusted God for the salvation of millions of souls.

At first I trust Him for one soul, then six, then ten souls, then hundreds, thousands, millions, and most recently, for a billion souls for Christ. These goals are not built on careless presumptions or figures plucked out of the air in some kind of a mystical or emotional experience. But they are based upon my confidence in the sovereignty, holiness, love, wisdom, power, and grace of the omnipotent God. Because of His gracious blessing upon past efforts, I have undertaken great efforts for His glory and praise. No credit should be given to me or to the ministry of which I am a part, but only to the One in whom I place my faith.

Faith must have an object, and the object of my faith is God and His inspired Word. The right view of God generates faith. Faith is like a muscle; it grows with exercise (see Gal 3:11). The more we see God accomplish in and through our lives, the more we can be assured that He will accomplish as we trust and obey Him more.

President Ronald Reagan signed a proclamation naming 1983 as the "Year of the Bible." He was joined by Senator William L. Armstrong, Dr. William R. Bright, and Rep. Carlos J. Moorhead.

Photograph: United Press International

112 – The Struggle Within

Once a new Christian went to a missionary for counsel. He was very much troubled by the spiritual conflict going on within his heart. He wanted to do what God wanted him to do, but he was frequently disobeying God. He found that he was prone to do evil things, even as he did before he became a Christian.

The man described this conflict within himself as a dogfight. "It is as though I have two dogs inside me fighting each other constantly."

The missionary asked him, "Which dog wins the fight?"

After several moments of silence, the man said, "The dog that wins is the one I tell to sic 'em."

Man has a free will; he is a free moral agent. He can decide, even as a Spirit-filled Christian, whether he will obey the dictates of the flesh (the carnal desires) or a leading of the Spirit. Whether he lives a consistent, Spirit-filled life is determined by the frequency with which he says "Yes" to the leading of the Spirit and "No" to the temptations of the flesh.

As long as we walk around in fleshly bodies here on planet earth, in Satan's domain, we will never be free from the pressures of these negative forces. The Bible says, "The heart is the most deceitful thing there is, and desperately wicked" (Jer 17:9, TLB). Therefore, I cannot hope to make myself good enough to earn God's favor. The only way I can please God is to trust Him to enable me to be obedient to His will.

113 – Beyond "Churchianity"

Recently Vonette and I were in Switzerland, where I spoke to businessmen and several churches. While we were there, God spoke to me of the urgency for every believer to live a Christian life that is worth sharing. I was surrounded by wonderful people who call themselves Christians: They go to church, they have been baptized, but Jesus is not a reality to many of them. One of the difficulties of ministry in Switzerland is to help people realize the difference between biblical Christianity and the "churchianity" of this country and much of Western Europe.

J.B. Phillips' says in his introduction to the New Testament Epistles, "There is a vast difference between the Christianity of the 20th century and the first century. To us, Christianity is all too often a code of ethics, a philosophy of life, a standard of performance. But to those first-century it was a new quality of life altogether. They did not hesitate to describe this as Christ living in them.... Perhaps if we believed what they believed, we could achieve what they achieved."

We all need to ask ourselves this question: Is my brand of Christianity worth sharing? I long that everything about my life—attitudes, actions, motives, desires, and words—will bring praise to our great God. I pray that no one would hear us speak or witness without knowing God sent us. Jesus gives us the secret, as recorded in John 15. We are to abide in our Lord and have His Word abide in us.

114 – A Formula for Spiritual Revolution

Not long ago, I awoke with a message running through my mind. I was unable to go back to sleep. So I got up and wrote down the following thoughts to share with any sincere believer in Christ who really wants his life to be maximized for His glory.

A Proven Formula for Spiritual Revolution: A humble, surrendered, and teachable spirit plus a growing knowledge of and obedience to God and His Word will, through the enabling of the Holy Spirit, result in a revolutionary, unprecedented spiritual harvest—personally, corporately as a movement, and worldwide for the glory of God.

If you analyze the "formula," you will see that God is calling us to humble ourselves. The number one sin robbing men and nations of God's great blessing is pride. We are to be yielded and teachable to do His will. God will use anyone who has that kind of attitude. At the same time, it is impossible to walk with God in intimacy and victory without hiding the Word of God in our hearts daily. Just as physical food is absolutely essential for physical health, so is spiritual food for our spirits.

If we meet the conditions of 2 Chronicles 7:14, God will enable us to become revolutionaries, and we will experience a spiritual harvest unlike anything we have ever seen. The contributions we make to the cause of Christ will help accelerate the day when everyone on planet Earth will have a chance to say yes to Jesus.

115 – Why Does God Want Our Love?

The question may come to your mind: "Why does God want our love?" From a human standpoint, this could appear selfish and egotistical. But God in His sovereignty and love has so created man that he finds his greatest joy and fulfillment when he loves God with all his heart and soul and mind and his neighbor as himself.

Early in my Christian life, I was troubled over the command to love God so completely. How could I ever measure up to such a high standard? Two very important considerations have helped me to want to love Him completely.

First, the Holy Spirit has filled my heart with God's love, as promised in the Scriptures. "For we know how dearly God loves us, and we feel this warm love everywhere within us because God has given us the Holy Spirit to fill our hearts with His love" (Rom 5:5, TLB).

Second, by meditating on the wonderful things God has done and is doing for me, I find my love for Him growing. I love Him because He first loved me (see 1 Jn 4:19).

We are to love God, our neighbors, our enemies, and our family members. And, we are to love ourselves with God's kind of love. We are to give God our first love, never allowing anyone or anything to come before Him. But, supernaturally, we are to express unconditional love to others—a love no less in its quality and magnitude than that which we express toward God.

116 – Joy: Love's Strength

Recently, I was explaining to a group of Christians the meaning of Proverbs 15:13–15: "A happy face means a glad heart, a sad face means a breaking heart. When a man is gloomy, everything seems to go wrong and when he is cheerful everything seems right" (TLB).

Paul tells us the source of joy is the Holy Spirit (see 1 Thes 1:6). So if a man is filled with the Spirit, he will have a joyful heart. When we are filled with the Spirit, we will express love by singing and making melody in our hearts to the Lord. A happy heart will inevitably express a joyful countenance.

If we do not have a joyful, peaceful countenance, there is reason to question whether we have a loving, joyful heart. And if we do not have a loving joyful heart, it is not likely that we are filled with the Spirit.

One of the Christian leaders listening to me approached me later. He just happened to have a somber, stern appearance. He explained to me that this was a new concept to him, and since he was reared in another culture, he felt that his somber countenance was a cultural thing.

We analyzed the Scripture together and concluded that culture has nothing to do with this. If we truly understand the Spirit-filled life, whatever our cultural background, the joy of the Lord will flow from us—from our "innermost being shall flow rivers of living water" (Jn 7:38, NAS).

117 – Not Forgotten by God

I am glad God knows everything about us, aren't you? If He could forget something, it might be you or me! But He will never forget us. He even keeps an account of the number of hairs on our heads. God promises through Isaiah:

"Can a mother forget the baby at her breast and have no compassion on the child she has borne? Though she may forget, I will not forget you! See, I have engraved you on the palms of my hands" (Is 49:15,16, NIV).

The reference to the engraving on the palms of God's hands is a prophecy about the death of Christ on the cross when the Roman soldiers drove nails through His hands. Christ submitted to death because of His love for us; the nail holes are eternal reminders of that love. No wonder we can have assurance that God will never forget about us!

Consider a few things that demonstrate how well God knows you.

- *God knows how you are designed.*
- *God knows everything about your past.*
- *God knows the challenges you face in your current situation.*
- *God knows the future He wants for you.*
- *God knows what choices will lead to His best for you.*

As you reflect on the fact that God knows all about you, your joys, your sorrows, your disobedience, open your heart to Him and follow Him. He will help you live victoriously in the knowledge that He knows all about you and loves you unconditionally.

118 – The Power of God's Holiness

Anyone who has been near a wildfire understands its tremendous power. When it roars through an area, everything is changed. Ancient trees are diminished to cinders. Buildings are reduced to rubble. Nothing can withstand its fury. Wildfires also bring new growth and regeneration.

In the Bible, God's holiness is sometimes pictured as a fire. A.W. Tozer writes:

Only fire can give even a remote conception of it. In fire He appeared at the burning bush; in the pillar of fire He dwelt through all the long wilderness journey. The fire that glowed between the wings of the cherubim in the holy place was called the Shekinah, the Presence, through the years of Israel's glory, and when the Old have given place to the New, He came at Pentecost as a fiery flame and rested upon each disciple.*

What does a fire do? It destroys the dead, purifies the impurities, and transforms the landscape. It is at the same time powerful, beautiful, and awesome.

God's holiness has great power. Moses asked, "Who else among the gods is like you, O Lord? Who is glorious in holiness like you—so awesome in splendor, performing such wonders?" (Ex 15:11, NLT). Nothing compares to the splendor of His holiness. His moral excellence is the absolute standard of integrity and ethical purity for all within His universe. God's supreme holiness infinitely sets Him apart from His creation. His holiness never diminishes.

* A.W. Tozer, *The Pursuit of God* (Camp Hill, PA; Christian Publications, 1993), 37.

India, 1987

119 – Give God Reverential Respect

Many Scripture passages tell us to fear God. King David tells us, "Serve the Lord with reverent fear, and rejoice with trembling" (Ps 2:11, NLT). Solomon wrote, "The fear of the Lord is the beginning of wisdom, and knowledge of the Holy One is understanding" (Prv 9:10, NIV). This fear does not mean to be afraid of God, but rather to express reverential awe before Him. God is not the "man upstairs." He is the great, holy, righteous, omnipotent, loving, creator God.

A couple of years ago, I was privileged to receive the prestigious Templeton award for the advancement of religion. As part of the honor, Vonette and I went to Buckingham Palace to meet with Prince Philip. Because we were meeting royalty, we were very conscious of our appearance and our behavior.

Do we have less concern when we come before our Sovereign God, the ruler of the universe? He deserves even more reverence and respect than any human being. Our holy God is always worthy of our highest respect.

It is the desire of my heart to be holy as He is holy and never ever to disappoint Him in any way. I would rather die than bring dishonor to His holy name.

I encourage you to examine how you come before God, how you treat His name before others, and how you respect His Word. In your daily quiet time with Him, give Him the honor He deserves. Spend more time worshiping Him than asking for your own needs.

120 – God Knows Everything

What would your life be like if you were considered one of the most brilliant minds in the world? Many of us think of Albert Einstein when we think about the most dazzling intellects. Did you know that the beginnings of his theory of relativity came from an essay that he wrote when he was sixteen years old? By age twenty-six, he had published five major research papers in an important German journal. For one of those papers, he received his doctorate. The ideas he introduced in these papers were so revolutionary that they changed the way we view the scientific universe.

But God knows everything. He is the only source of all true knowledge, understanding, and wisdom, everything we know and understand originated with Him. Isaiah tellingly asks:

> Who has understood the mind of the Lord, or instructed him as his counselor? Whom did the Lord consult to enlighten him, and who taught him the right way? Who was it that taught him knowledge or showed him the path of understanding? (Is 40:13,14, NIV).

What great news! We do not need an intellect like Einstein's. We know Someone who knows the answers to all life's questions. "Oh, the depth of the riches of the wisdom and knowledge of God! How unsearchable his judgments, and his paths beyond tracing out! Who has known the mind of the Lord? Or who has been his counselor?" (Rom 11:33,34, NIV).